# PERFECTION
# PENDING

# PERFECTION

# PENDING

## AND OTHER FAVORITE

## DISCOURSES

RUSSELL M. NELSON

DESERET BOOK COMPANY

SALT LAKE CITY, UTAH

**Library of Congress Cataloging-in-Publication Data**

Nelson, Russell Marion.
   Perfection pending, and other favorite discourses / Russell M. Nelson.
     p.   cm.
   Includes bibliographical references and index.
   ISBN 1-57345-405-2 (hb)
    1. Church of Jesus Christ of Latter-day Saints—Sermons.
   2. Mormon Church—Sermons. 3. Sermons, American.  I. Title.
BX8639.N45P47    1998
252'.09332—dc21
                                           98-24542
                                            CIP

Printed in the United States of America          18961-6361

10   9   8   7   6   5   4   3   2   1

# CONTENTS

CONTENTS

**PART 3: CHRIST AND THE COVENANT**

# PART 1

---

# PERFECTION
# PENDING

# PERFECTION PENDING

_____

If I were to ask which of the Lord's commandments is most difficult to keep, many of us might cite Matthew 5:48: "Be ye therefore perfect, even as your Father which is in heaven is perfect."[1]

Keeping this commandment can be a concern because each of us is far from perfect, both spiritually and temporally. Reminders come repeatedly. We may lock keys inside the car, or even forget where the car is parked. And not infrequently, we walk intently from one part of the house to another, only to forget the reason for the errand.

When we compare our personal performance with the supreme standard of the Lord's expectation, the reality of imperfection can at times be depressing. My heart goes out to conscientious Saints who, because of their shortcomings, allow feelings of depression to rob them of happiness in life.

We all need to remember: men are that they might have joy—not guilt trips![2] We also need to remember that the Lord gives no commandments that are impossible to obey. But sometimes we fail to comprehend them fully.

Our understanding of perfection might be aided if we classify it into two categories. The first could pertain uniquely to this

3

life—*mortal* perfection. The second category could pertain uniquely to the next life—*immortal* or *eternal* perfection.

## MORTAL PERFECTION

In this life, certain actions can be perfected. A baseball pitcher can throw a no-hit, no-run ball game. A surgeon can perform an operation without an error. A musician can render a selection without a mistake. One can likewise achieve perfection in being punctual, paying tithing, keeping the Word of Wisdom, and so on. The enormous effort required to attain such self-mastery is rewarded with a deep sense of satisfaction. More importantly, spiritual attainments in mortality accompany us into eternity.[3]

James gave a practical standard by which mortal perfection could be measured. He said, "If any man offend not in word, the same is a *perfect* man."[4]

Scriptures have described Noah, Seth, and Job as *perfect* men.[5] No doubt the same term might apply to a large number of faithful disciples in various dispensations. Alma said that "there were many, exceedingly great many,"[6] who were pure before the Lord.

This does not mean that these people never made mistakes or never had need of correction. The process of perfection includes challenges to overcome and steps to repentance that may be very painful.[7] There is a proper place for chastisement in the molding of character, for we know that "whom the Lord loveth he chasteneth."[8]

Mortal perfection can be achieved as we try to perform every duty, keep every law, and strive to be as perfect in our sphere as our Heavenly Father is in His. If we do the best we can, the Lord will bless us according to our deeds and the desires of our hearts.[9]

### ETERNAL PERFECTION

But Jesus asked for more than mortal perfection. The moment He uttered the words "even as your Father which is in heaven is perfect," He raised our sights beyond the bounds of mortality. Our Heavenly Father has eternal perfection. This very fact merits a much broader perspective.

Recently, I studied the English and Greek editions of the New Testament, concentrating on each use of the term *perfect* and its derivatives. Studying both languages together provided some interesting insights, since Greek was the original language of the New Testament.

In Matthew 5:48, the term *perfect* was translated from the Greek *teleios,* which means "complete." *Teleios* is an adjective derived from the noun *telos,* which means "end."[10] The infinitive form of the verb is *teleiono,* which means "to reach a distant end, to be fully developed, to consummate, or to finish."[11] Please note that the word does not imply "freedom from error"; it implies "achieving a distant objective." In fact, when writers of the Greek New Testament wished to describe perfection of behavior—precision or excellence of human effort—they did *not* employ a form of *teleios*; instead, they chose different words.[12]

*Teleios* is not a total stranger to us. From it comes the prefix *tele-* that we use every day. *Telephone* literally means "distant talk." *Television* means "to see distantly." *Telephoto* means "distant light," and so on.

With that background in mind, let us consider another highly significant statement made by the Lord. Just prior to His crucifixion, He said that on "the third day I *shall be perfected.*"[13] Think of that! The sinless, errorless Lord—already perfect by our mortal standards—proclaimed His own state of perfection yet to be in the future.[14] His *eternal* perfection would follow His resurrection and receipt of "all power . . . in heaven and in earth."[15]

The perfection that the Savior envisions for us is much more than errorless performance. It is the eternal expectation as expressed by the Lord in His great intercessory prayer to His Father—that we might be made perfect and be able to dwell with them in the eternities ahead.[16]

The Lord's entire work and glory pertains to the immortality and eternal life of each human being.[17] He came into the world to do the will of His Father, who sent Him.[18] His sacred responsibility was foreseen before the Creation[19] and was foretold by all His holy prophets since the world began.[20]

The atonement of Christ fulfilled the long-awaited purpose for which He had come to the earth. His concluding words upon Calvary's cross referred to the culmination of His assignment—to atone for all humankind. Then He said, "It is finished."[21] Not surprisingly, the Greek word from which *finished* was derived is *teleios*.

That Jesus attained eternal perfection *following* His resurrection is confirmed in the Book of Mormon. It records the visit of the resurrected Lord to the people of ancient America. There He repeated the important injunction previously cited, but with one very significant addition. He said, "I would that ye should be perfect *even as I,* or your Father who is in heaven is perfect."[22] This time He listed Himself along with His Father as a perfected personage. Previously, He had not.[23]

Resurrection is requisite for eternal perfection. Thanks to the atonement of Jesus Christ, our bodies, corruptible in mortality, will become incorruptible. Our physical frames, now subject to disease, death, and decay, will acquire immortal glory.[24] Presently sustained by the blood of life[25] and ever aging, our

6

bodies will be sustained by spirit and become changeless and beyond the bounds of death.[26]

Eternal perfection is reserved for those who overcome all things and inherit the fulness of the Father in His heavenly mansions. Perfection consists in gaining eternal life—the kind of life that God lives.[27]

## ORDINANCES AND COVENANTS OF THE TEMPLE

Scriptures identify other important prerequisites to eternal perfection. They relate to the ordinances and covenants of the temple.[28] No accountable individual can receive exaltation in the celestial kingdom without the ordinances of the temple. Endowments and sealings are for our personal perfection and are secured through our faithfulness.[29]

This requirement also pertains to our ancestors. Paul taught "that they without us should not be made *perfect.*"[30] Again, in that verse, the Greek term from which *perfect* was translated was a form of *teleios.*[31]

In latter-day revelation, the Lord was even more explicit. His prophet wrote: "My dearly beloved brethren and sisters, let me assure you that these are principles in relation to the dead and the living that cannot be lightly passed over, as pertaining to our salvation. For their salvation is necessary and essential to our salvation. . . . They without us cannot be made perfect—neither can we without our dead be made perfect."[32]

## ENCOURAGEMENT FROM THE SAVIOR'S EXAMPLE

Our climb up the path to perfection is aided by encouragement from the scriptures. They hold the promise that we shall, if faithful in all things, become like Deity. John the beloved Apostle wrote:

7

"We should be called the sons [and daughters] of God. . . .

". . . When he shall appear, we shall be like him; for we shall see him as he is.

"And every man that hath this hope in him purifieth himself, even as he is pure."[33]

Continuing encouragement comes as we follow the example of Jesus, who taught, "Be ye holy; for I am holy."[34] His hope for us is crystal clear! He declared: "What manner of men ought ye to be? Verily I say unto you, even as I am."[35] Thus, our adoration of Jesus is best expressed by our emulation of Jesus.[36]

People have never failed to follow Jesus because His standards were imprecise or insufficiently high. Quite to the contrary. Some have disregarded His teachings because they were viewed as being too precise or impractically high! Yet such lofty standards, when earnestly pursued, produce great inner peace and incomparable joy.

There is no other individual to compare with Jesus Christ, nor is there any other exhortation equal to His sublime expression of hope: "I would that ye should be perfect even as I, or your Father who is in heaven is perfect."[37]

This divine entreaty is consistent with the fact that, as begotten children of heavenly parents, we are endowed with the potential to become like them, just as mortal children may become like their mortal parents.

The Lord restored His church to help us prepare for perfection. Paul said that the Savior placed in the Church Apostles, prophets, and teachers, "for the perfecting of the saints, . . . for the edifying of the body of Christ:

"Till we all come in the unity of the faith, and of the knowledge of the Son of God, unto a *perfect* man, unto the measure of the stature of the fulness of Christ."[38]

The *perfect* man described in Paul's quotation is the completed person—*teleios*—the glorified soul!

Moroni taught how to gain this glorious objective. His instruction stands in any age as an antidote for depression and a prescription for joy. I echo his plea: "Come unto Christ, and be perfected in him, and deny yourselves of all ungodliness; . . . love God with all your might, mind and strength, then . . . ye may be perfect in Christ . . . holy, [and] without spot."[39]

Meanwhile, let us do the best we can and try to improve each day. When our imperfections appear, we can keep trying to correct them. We can be more forgiving of flaws in ourselves and among those we love. We can be comforted and forbearing. The Lord taught, "Ye are not able to abide the presence of God now . . . ; wherefore, continue in patience until ye are perfected."[40]

We need not be dismayed if our earnest efforts toward perfection now seem so arduous and endless. Perfection is pending. It can come in full only after the Resurrection and only through the Lord. It awaits all who love Him and keep His commandments. It includes thrones, kingdoms, principalities, powers, and dominions.[41] It is the end for which we are to endure.[42] It is the eternal perfection that God has in store for each of us.

NOTES

1. Those words were given additional intensity in the Joseph Smith Translation: "Ye are therefore commanded to be perfect, even as your Father who is in heaven is perfect" (JST, Matthew 5:50).

2. See 2 Nephi 2:25.

3. See D&C 130:18–19.

4. James 3:2; emphasis added.

5. See Genesis 6:9; D&C 107:43; Job 1:1.

6. Alma 13:12.

7. See Hebrews 5:8.

8. Hebrews 12:6.

9. See D&C 137:9.

10. Incidentally, the feminine form of this noun is *teleia,* the Greek term for a period at the *end* of a sentence.

11. Footnote *b* for Matthew 5:48 states: "GR complete, finished, fully developed" (LDS edition of the King James Version of the Bible [Salt Lake City: The Church of Jesus Christ of Latter-day Saints, 1979], 1195).

12. A few examples include:

• "Out of the mouth of babes and sucklings thou hast *perfected* praise" (Matthew 21:16; emphasis added).

• "The disciple is not above his master: but every one that is *perfect* shall be as his master" (Luke 6:40). In both of these verses, *perfect* came from the Greek term *katartizo,* which means "to fit out, equip, put in order, arrange, adjust; to fit or frame for one's self"—an act of preparation.

• Another speaks of "*perfect* understanding" (Luke 1:3; emphasis added). In this instance, *perfect* came from the Greek adverb *akribos,* which means "exactly, accurately."

• Another verse refers to those who touched the hem of the Master's garment and "were made *perfectly* whole" (Matthew 14:36; emphasis added). *Perfect* in this instance came from the Greek *diasozo,* which means "to preserve through danger, to bring safely through, to save, keep from perishing, to rescue."

13. Luke 13:32; emphasis added.

14. In the Greek text of that proclamation, the verb *teleiono* was again used, in its *future* tense—*teleiouma.*

15. Matthew 28:18; see also D&C 93:2–22.

16. See John 17:23–24.

17. See Moses 1:39.

18. See 3 Nephi 27:13.

19. See Moses 4:1–2; 7:62; Abraham 3:22–28.

20. See Acts 3:19–21.

21. John 19:30. In modern revelation, Jesus used similar language. He said, "I partook and *finished* my preparations unto the children of men" (D&C 19:19; emphasis added).

10

22. 3 Nephi 12:48; emphasis added.

23. See Matthew 5:48.

24. See Alma 11:45; D&C 76:64–70.

25. See Leviticus 17:11.

26. Bible Dictionary, "Resurrection," 761: "A resurrection means to become immortal, without blood, yet with a body of flesh and bone."

27. See Joseph Fielding Smith, *The Way to Perfection* (Independence, Missouri: The Genealogical Society of Utah, 1946), 331; Bruce R. McConkie, *Mormon Doctrine,* 2d ed. (Salt Lake City: Bookcraft, 1966), 237.

28. Joseph Smith taught, "Being born again, comes by the Spirit of God through ordinances" (*Teachings of the Prophet Joseph Smith,* sel. Joseph Fielding Smith [Salt Lake City: Deseret Book Co., 1938], 162).

29. See Joseph Fielding Smith, *Doctrines of Salvation,* comp. Bruce R. McConkie, 3 vols. (Salt Lake City: Bookcraft, 1954–56), 2:45.

30. Hebrews 11:40; emphasis added.

31. *teleioo.*

32. D&C 128:15; see also *Teachings of the Prophet Joseph Smith,* 159.

33. 1 John 3:1–3. For additional commentary, see Joseph Fielding Smith, *The Way to Perfection,* 7–9.

34. 1 Peter 1:16; see also Leviticus 11:44–45; 19:2; 20:26.

35. 3 Nephi 27:27.

36. See Neal A. Maxwell, *We Talk of Christ, We Rejoice in Christ* (Salt Lake City: Deseret Book Co., 1984), 145; Hugh B. Brown, *The Abundant Life* (Salt Lake City: Bookcraft, 1965), 199.

37. 3 Nephi 12:48.

38. Ephesians 4:12–13; emphasis added.

39. Moroni 10:32–33.

40. D&C 67:13.

41. See D&C 132:19.

42. This concept is supported by the fact that in verses of the New Testament that refer to the *end* for which we are to endure, the Greek word from which *end* was translated was also derived from *telos* (see Matthew 10:22; 24:13; Mark 13:13).

11

# SPIRITUAL CAPACITY

A verse of scripture opens a door of opportunity for each of us: "There is a spirit in man," said Job, "and the inspiration of the Almighty giveth them understanding."[1] To take advantage of such an opportunity, we need more than a verbal incentive. We need an example—someone to show us how spiritual capacity can be developed. I have selected as an example President Gordon B. Hinckley.[2] My motive in doing so is not one of adulation, but of emulation. We can draw upon his example in order to improve our own spiritual attributes.

During 1997, Sister Nelson and I had the privilege of accompanying President and Sister Hinckley to eleven countries[3] for which I have had some responsibilities. That gave us a rare opportunity to observe him closely under a variety of conditions. His teachings are always inspiring and relevant. They should be studied carefully and applied individually. They represent the word of the Lord for His people.[4]

But my purpose is not to review the content of President Hinckley's messages. Instead, I would like to focus upon his spiritual capacities. He has developed many, including "faith, virtue, knowledge, temperance, patience, brotherly kindness, godliness, charity, humility, [and] diligence."[5]

His humility, for example, is so sincere that he would have me point only to the Lord Jesus Christ as our great exemplar.[6] Of course, He is! The Master said, "I have given you an example, that ye should do as I have done."[7] We must never lose sight of the Savior's enduring standard as the ultimate for each of us.

But we can also learn much from a man who has spent his entire lifetime in striving to be more like the Lord. On 23 June 1910, Gordon B. Hinckley was born, and the infant was cradled in the arms of his loving parents. That newborn babe looked much like any other, I presume. An infant's body is tiny, and its spiritual capacities are undeveloped. While the body may reach the peak of its maturation in a few years, the development of the spirit may never reach the limit of its capacity, because there is no end to progression.

President Hinckley's personality, manner, and native intelligence have always been uniquely his. To these inborn attributes, however, he has added spiritual capacities, and they are continuing to increase.

Both his parents and he understood the importance of education and a mission. After his graduation from the university, he faced a major decision in 1933, when he was called to go on a mission. At that time, most young men in the Church were not able to serve because of a global economic depression that deprived nearly everyone of available cash. Earlier, his wonderful mother, with foresight and faith, had established a small savings account for his mission. Though she died before his call, her fund sent him on his way.

Shortly after Elder Hinckley's labors began in England, he became discouraged and wrote to his father. After reading that letter, his father wrote a reply, which closed with these wise words: "Forget yourself and go to work."[8] Thanks to noble parents and a crucial decision to remain, Elder Hinckley completed his mission with honor. Now he often states that the good things that have happened to him since have all hinged upon that decision to stay. On his mission, he developed good habits of study, work, communication, budgeting, time management, and more. There he learned that nothing is too hard for the Lord.[9]

Long ago, President Hinckley harnessed the power of prayer. I have watched him pray over many weighty matters and receive inspired answers. Prayer invites those ennobling attributes of the Spirit that are ultimately "bestowed upon all who are true followers of . . . Jesus Christ."[10]

Hobbies can aid in spiritual development. Worthy music, dance, art, and writing are among the creative activities that can enrich the soul. A good hobby can dispel heartache and give zest to life.[11] Through the years, one of President Hinckley's hobbies has been his home. As a young father, he learned how to build. He acquired the skills necessary to remodel a house and make needed repairs. And more important, he has built and maintained the trust of his wife and their children. Together they have established—and are still adding to—wonderful memories with their children and grandchildren, who know that they are part of "a chosen generation . . . called . . . out of darkness into [the] marvellous light"[12] of the Lord. From the Hinckleys' parental example, we can learn a great lesson. Love at home comes when companions cultivate their commitment to keep the commandments of God.

President Hinckley's love of learning is catalyzed by curiosity. He grasps every opportunity to learn from others. On one occasion, I heard him quiz a local security officer for nearly an hour regarding crime control in a major city. I have heard him converse with building contractors, reporters, and those who specialize in the arts, architecture, business, government, law, medicine, and other disciplines. He knows their vocabularies, their challenges, and their strengths.

He has gained his remarkable ability as a writer by living close to the Spirit. Similar skills can come to others too, for scriptures state that such has been "given unto as many as called upon God to write by the spirit of inspiration."[13]

Through the years, President Hinckley has developed a remarkable sense of humor. You have heard his quip that "Sister Hinckley and I are learning that the so-called golden years are laced with lead."[14] I might add a pun. We are grateful to be led by that kind of lead. It gives ballast to balance one who might lean too far in any direction. And it gives stability to character.

While I focus upon President Hinckley, Sister Hinckley should also be included. They have been married for more than sixty years and have long been one in spirit, while maintaining their individuality. They do not waste time pondering the past or fretting about the future. And they persevere in spite of adversity.

While they were traveling from a chapel to an airport in Central America, their vehicle was involved in an accident. Sister Nelson and I were traveling behind them and saw it occur. A truck loaded on top with unsecured metal rods approached them at an intersection. To avoid a collision, its driver suddenly stopped the truck—inadvertantly launching those iron rods like javelins and piercing the Hinckleys' car. Windows were smashed; fenders and doors were dented. The accident could have been very serious. While shattered glass was being removed from their clothing and skin, President Hinckley said: "Thank the Lord for His blessing; now let's continue on in another car."

Among President Hinckley's spiritual attributes is that of compassion. He is sympathetic to people and feels a strong urge to help them. I have watched him weep with those who mourn and rejoice when Saints are blessed. Such compassion can come to anyone whose heart has truly been touched by the Spirit of the Lord.

President and Sister Hinckley have demonstrated that the capacity to understand increases as one learns and then teaches with diligence.[15] Unless illness interferes, age does not diminish—it augments—the capacity for spiritual development.

Each President of the Church, armed with the Holy Ghost as a constant companion, inherits an enormous workload at an age when most men would be retired. President Hinckley sets a pace that is unprecedented. In 1996, he visited missionaries, members, and friends of the Church in twenty-three nations on four continents. During that year, he gave more than 200 major discourses. His stride since that time continues to follow that same pattern. His strenuous schedule is driven by his determination to be "anxiously engaged"[16] in building the kingdom of God. Often I have heard him say, "I don't know how to get anything done except getting on my knees and pleading for help and then getting on my feet and going to work." Unshakable faith, hard work, and contagious optimism epitomize our prophet.

I have watched President Hinckley, in speaking before great congregations, depend upon the Holy Ghost, who serves "to enlighten and ennoble the mind, to purify and sanctify the soul, to incite to good works, and to reveal the things of God."[17]

President Hinckley has achieved spiritual supremacy over physical feelings. Even when entitled to normal complaints of "jet lag" or "burnout," he is attentive. I believe that his personal antidote for fatigue is enthusiasm[18] for the work. He is energized by the Lord, who said, "I will impart unto you of my Spirit, which shall enlighten your mind . . . [and] fill your soul with joy."[19]

One of our most memorable experiences occurred when we visited the temple construction site in Guayaquil, Ecuador. There

President Hinckley recounted to us how that property was selected. On a prior visit, he had been shown several possible locations, but none seemed to satisfy him. While prayerfully searching, he asked about ground on a hill not far from the airport. But it was said to be *not* for sale. President Hinckley directed that they visit that property anyway. There he received inspiration from the Almighty that this was the right place for the temple. Now we were privileged to stand on that spot reserved by the Lord and then procured for this sacred purpose. Our joy was indescribable.

The prophet makes major decisions on a daily basis. This he does with great capacity. Meanwhile, he encourages each of us to make choices that will "give us growth and joy in this life and eternal life in the world to come."[20]

This President of the Church calls many people to serve, knowing that much is required of them. He is keenly aware of their opportunities and risks. "Yes, this work requires sacrifice," he said. "It requires effort, it means courage to speak out and faith to try. . . . It needs men and women of solemn purpose."[21] "We know that there are some limits on what you can do, but we know also that there need be no limits on enthusiasm, planning, thoughtful consideration, and effort."[22]

Brothers and sisters, the spirit that dwells within each of us can be enriched with enthusiasm and enlightened by the Almighty. The process of spiritual growth is revealed in the scriptures: "Intelligence cleaveth unto intelligence; wisdom receiveth wisdom; truth embraceth truth; . . . [and] light cleaveth unto light."[23] "That which is of God is light; and he that receiveth light, and continueth in God, receiveth more light; and that light groweth brighter and brighter until the perfect day."[24]

Gratefully, we follow prophets who have been given a divine commission: "Whatsoever they shall speak when moved upon by

17

the Holy Ghost shall be scripture, shall be the will of the Lord, shall be the mind of the Lord, shall be the word of the Lord, shall be the voice of the Lord, and the power of God unto salvation."[25]

While we follow prophetic teachings, we can develop our spiritual capacities by emulating one such as President Gordon B. Hinckley. I thank God for this prophet. He is the Lord's anointed. Willingly I follow him. I love him and sustain him.

NOTES

1. Job 32:8. The word *spirit* in this verse was translated from the Hebrew noun *ruwach,* which means "wind, air, breath, mind, or spirit." The Greek noun for *spirit* is *pneuma.* It is the root from which English words such as *pneumatic* tires and *pneumonia* are derived. *Pneuma* also means "air, breath, mind, or spirit." It is used 385 times in the Greek New Testament.

2. Twenty-four years ago, Elder Gordon B. Hinckley was impressed to speak of his experiences accompanying President Harold B. Lee to nations abroad (see "We Thank Thee, O God, for a Prophet," *Ensign,* January 1974, 122–25).

3. United States of America, Panama, Nicaragua, Costa Rica, Honduras, El Salvador, Guatemala, Uruguay, Paraguay, Ecuador, and Venezuela.

4. See Amos 3:7; D&C 68:4.

5. D&C 4:6.

6. Among the many scriptural commandments, see 3 Nephi 27:27; Mormon 7:10.

7. John 13:15. If we love Him, we will keep His commandments (see Exodus 20:6; Deuteronomy 5:10; John 14:15; D&C 124:87).

8. See Sheri L. Dew, *Go Forward with Faith: The Biography of Gordon B. Hinckley* (Salt Lake City: Deseret Book Co., 1996), 64.

9. See Jeremiah 32:17; Luke 1:37.

10. Moroni 7:48.

11. See Richard G. Scott, "Finding Joy in Life," *Ensign,* May 1996, 25–26.

12. 1 Peter 2:9.

13. Moses 6:5; see also JST, Genesis 6:5.

14. "This Is the Work of the Master," *Ensign,* May 1995, 70.

15. See D&C 88:78.

16. D&C 58:27.

17. James E. Talmage, *The Articles of Faith,* 12th ed. (Salt Lake City: The Deseret News, 1924), 167; see also D&C 121:26.

18. The word *enthusiasm* comes from Greek roots *en,* meaning "in," and *theos,* meaning "God"—"God within us."

19. D&C 11:13; see also D&C 124:88.

20. "Caesar, Circus, or Christ?" in *Brigham Young University Speeches of the Year* (26 October 1965), 8.

21. In Conference Report, October 1969, 115.

22. Bonneville International Corporation Management Seminar, 23 February 1992.

23. D&C 88:40.

24. D&C 50:24.

25. D&C 68:4.

# INTEGRITY OF HEART

The mitral valve, one of four valves within the heart, is a delicate and durable structure situated between the left atrium and the left ventricle. It is a check valve, regulating the flow of freshly oxygenated blood from the lungs to the heart's powerful pump. The heart's mitral valve opens and closes about one hundred thousand times a day—36 million times each year. It consists of soft, billowing tissue, cords, and attachments.

In a way, the mitral valve is like a parachute. When in operation, a parachute's sail billows to form a pocket of resistance that slows the descent of the passenger tethered to it by strong cords. Similarly, the mitral valve opens widely to let blood enter the pump, then snaps securely shut when blood is ejected from the heart. The work of the heart goes on day after day, year after year, with or without our awareness.

But things can go wrong with the mitral valve. If for any reason it doesn't close completely, blood is regurgitated backwards. The high pressure exerted by the heart is then impelled directly toward the lungs. If that were to go on very long, the heart and lungs would fail. From my experience as a cardiac surgeon, I know that this problem may occur if one of the mitral valve's cords ruptures spontaneously. When that occurs, stress on adjoining cords is immediately increased and the neighboring cords are much more prone to rupture. When the cords break, the entire mitral valve loses its integrity, and a life is in serious jeopardy.

Cardiac surgeons speak of the heart in terms of its structural integrity. The word *integrity* is related to the word *integer,* which means "entire" or "whole." Integrity may be defined as "the state of being unimpaired." Integrity also means "incorruptibility"—a firm adherence to a code of values. Integrity denotes a state of completeness. If any component of the heart loses its integrity, the heart is impaired and a vicious cycle ensues. An anatomical flaw leads to improper function, and improper function leads to further failure. Therefore, the ultimate objective of any cardiac operation is to restore structural integrity to the heart.

## STRUCTURAL, TEMPORAL, AND SPIRITUAL LAWS

Why do I use such a teaching model? The reason comes from scripture. The Lord said, "All things unto me are spiritual, and not at any time have I given unto you a law which was temporal."[1] Thus, temporal or physical laws that relate to our divine creation often have a spiritual application. This should come as no surprise, because "all [of God's] kingdoms have a law given. . . .

"And unto every kingdom is given a law; and unto every law there are certain bounds also and conditions."[2]

The Lord taught that anyone "who hath seen any or the least of these [kingdoms] hath seen God moving in his majesty and power."[3] Because He is the Creator of both the physical and spiritual components of our being, examples of the importance of *structural* integrity can teach much about the importance of *spiritual* integrity.

A model of spiritual integrity can be depicted using the mitral valve analogy. For example, let the sail of integrity,

21

tethered by cords, attach to us as individuals. Let us label each cord with a spiritual quality, such as specific attributes of character mentioned in the thirteenth article of faith—being honest, true, chaste, benevolent, virtuous, doing good, and seeking things of good report. Other qualities of character could be listed, but these will suffice to illustrate the principle. As we study this illustration, let us think of someone we admire greatly—someone with spiritual integrity. His or her integrity is characterized by the strength of each of these cords of character. As long as this model is unimpaired, the sail, cords, and attachments are all secure.

But imagine what would happen if one of the supporting cords breaks—the cord of honesty, for example. If that cord breaks, additional strain is immediately imposed on neighboring cords of chastity, virtue, and benevolence, in accordance with the law of sequential stress.

## WARNINGS AND EXPECTATIONS

In scripture, we have been warned of such risk:

"And there shall also be many which shall say: Eat, drink, and be merry; . . . yea, lie a little, take the advantage of . . . thy neighbor. . . .

"Yea, and there shall be many which shall teach after this manner, false and vain and foolish doctrines."[4]

Such doctrines are dangerous because they are hazardous to our precious integrity. Yet some people are so easily tempted to lie, to cheat, to steal, or to bear false witness—just a little. We cannot commit a little sin without being subject to the consequences. If we tolerate a little sin today, we tolerate a little more tomorrow, and before long, a cord of integrity is broken. Sequential stress will follow, putting adjacent cords at risk.

President Brigham Young had strong feelings about such matters. On one occasion, he said:

"Many want to shade a little, rather than to work hard for an honest living. Such practices must be put away, and this people must become sanctified in their affections to God, and learn to deal honestly, truly, and uprightly with one another in every respect, with all the integrity that fills the heart of an angel. They must learn to feel that they can trust all they possess with their brethren and sisters, saying, 'All I have I entrust to you: keep it until I call for it.' . . . That principle must prevail in the midst of this people: you must preserve your integrity to each other."[5]

President Young's statement strikes a sympathetic response in me when I reflect upon the days our nine daughters enjoyed as college students dating their boyfriends. As a young suitor would call at our door, I might silently ask myself: "Would he one day call me Dad?" "Would he help to care for me in my old age?" And sometimes I wondered—knowing well the history of Jacob, son of Isaac—whether any of these boyfriends would follow the biblical precedent of Jacob, who kissed Rachel as soon as they met.[6]

I trusted each young man to be a man of integrity. So I echo those thoughts expressed by President Young: "All I have I entrust to you: keep it until I call for it." Now, some years later, I am pleased to state that our nine sons-in-law have earned and have honored that trust we placed in them. Each one possesses integrity of heart, as do our daughters and our son.

Integrity safeguards love, and love makes family life rich and zestful—now and forever. But none of us is immune to temptation, and the adversary knows it. He would deceive, connive, or contrive any means to deprive us of potential joy and exaltation. He knows that if one little cord of control can be snapped, others likely will weaken later under increased strain. The result would be no integrity, no eternal life. Satan's triumph would be assured. If this domino-like deterioration causes a run in our spiritual stocking, qualities of character are lost and our cherished integrity is gone.

The Apostle Paul warned of the lethal wages of sin,[7] but the Savior didn't limit His caution to major transgression. He specifically warned against breaking "one of these least commandments."[8] His admonitions were meant to protect and preserve our precious integrity.

A surgeon can repair or replace a mitral valve that has lost its integrity. But no surgical procedure can be performed for loss of spiritual integrity of heart. Such breakdown is under individual control.

## SELF-ASSESSMENT AND REPAIR

The wise fisherman inspects his nets regularly. Should any flaw be detected, he repairs the defect without delay. An old saying teaches that "a stitch in time saves nine." Recorded revelation gives similar instruction. The Lord said, "Remember therefore from whence thou art fallen, and repent, and do the first works."[9]

If we are wise, we assess personal cords of integrity on a daily basis. We identify any weakness, and we repair it. Indeed, we have an obligation to do so. The words of Isaiah apply equally to all:

"Strengthen ye the weak hands, and confirm the feeble knees.

"Say to them that are of a fearful heart, Be strong."[10]

Private personal prayer is a good time for introspection. Morning prayer might include a petition for honesty, chastity, virtue, or for simply being of service to others. In the evening, there may be another quick checkup on all of those attributes. We pray for the preservation of our spiritual integrity, then we work for it. Should any flaw be found, we will want to begin the process of prompt repair that will protect further disintegration of a threatened spiritual quality.

Self-assessment is done best in many little steps, asking ourselves questions such as these:

• What do we do when we make a mistake? Do we admit our error and apologize, or do we deny it and blame others?

• What do we do when we are in a group where wrong ideas or activities are promoted? Do we endorse error by our silence, or do we take a stand?

• Are we totally true to our employers, or are we less than loyal?

• Do we keep the Sabbath day, obey the Word of Wisdom, honor our father and mother?

• If we have made sacred covenants in the temple, how do we react when we hear evil-speaking against the Lord's anointed? Do we honor all covenants made there? Or do we allow exceptions and rationalize our behavior to suit our preconceived preferences?

• How do we honor our word? Can our promises be trusted?

President Karl G. Maeser once said:

"I have been asked what I mean by word of honor. I will tell you. Place me behind prison walls—walls of stone ever so high, ever so thick, reaching ever so far into the ground—there is a possibility that in some way or another I may be able to escape; but stand me on the floor and draw a chalk line around me and have me give my word of honor never to cross it. Can I get out of that circle? No, never! I'd die first!"[11]

I agree with Brother Maeser. A promise is binding until we fulfill it or are released from it.

We should not be discouraged or depressed by our shortcomings. No one is without weakness. As part of the divine plan, we are tested to see whether we master weakness or let weakness master us. Proper diagnosis is essential to proper treatment. The Lord gave us this remarkable assurance: "Because thou hast seen thy weakness thou shalt be made strong."[12] But wishing for strength won't make us strong. It takes faith and work to shore up a weakened cord of integrity.

We know the process of self-repair called repentance. Mercifully, we do not have to begin that process alone. We can receive help through counsel with trusted family members and Church leaders. But their aid is more likely to help if we seek it not merely to satisfy a formality but with real intent to reform and come closer to Christ. He is the ultimate physician. Real faith in Him will provide real relief—and glorious rewards. He said, "Because thou hast seen thy weakness thou shalt be made strong, even unto the sitting down in the place which I have prepared in the mansions of my Father."[13]

Mistakes may mar our worthiest intentions, and serious sin can stain with scarlet the slate of pristine white that was once ours. As none of us may escape sin, none of us may escape suffering. Repentance may not be easy, but it is worth it. Repentance not only bleaches, it heals!

## TESTIMONY BUILDS STRENGTH

Now for some more good news: Not only can our integrity of heart be maintained, it can be strengthened. A testimony of the gospel is one of the most important fortifiers we know. So taught Elder Orson Pratt, who faced the burden of leadership imposed upon him. To know the truth for himself "required a witness independent of the testimony of others." So Brother Pratt once confided:

"I sought for this witness. I did not receive it immediately,

26

but when the Lord saw the integrity of my heart and the anxiety of my mind—when He saw that I was willing to travel hundreds of miles for the sake of learning the principles of the truth, He gave me a testimony for myself, which conferred upon me the most perfect knowledge that Joseph Smith was a true prophet, and that this book, called the Book of Mormon, was in reality a Divine revelation, and that God had once more, in reality, spoken to the human family. What joy this knowledge gave me! No language that I am acquainted with could describe the sensations I experienced when I received a knowledge from Heaven of the truth of this work."[14]

Just as Orson Pratt's unshakable testimony fortified him for great trials ahead, our personal testimony will strengthen us for future challenges. Challenges come to a heart surgeon every day. From many years of experience, I learned that the integrity of my team's performance was absolutely essential to the success of an operation. Any serious misstep, even unintentional, could nullify the fervent prayers of a patient even when fortified by great faith of family and friends. I learned that desired blessings come only when all necessary laws are obeyed. Hence, the demands of obedience can be painful. Sanctification is neither simple nor quick.

Speaking of His Saints in the latter days, the Lord said:

"They must needs be chastened and tried, even as Abraham, who was commanded to offer up his only son.

"For all those who will not endure chastening, but deny me, cannot be sanctified."[15]

If President Young could speak today, he might counsel us as he did in his day:

"In all your business transactions, words, and communications, if you commit [a wrong] act, repent of that immediately, and call upon God to deliver you from evil and give you the light of His spirit. Never do a thing that your conscience, and the light within you, tell you is wrong. Never do a wrong, but do all the good you possibly can. Never do a thing to mar the peaceable influence of the Holy Spirit in you; then whatever you are engaged in—whether in business, in the dance, or in the pulpit—you are ready to officiate at any time in any of the ordinances of the House of God. If I commit an overt act, the Lord knows of the integrity of my heart, and, through sincere repentance, He forgives me."[16]

President Young linked the integrity of his heart to forgiveness from the Lord. Forgiveness can be earned only through full repentance. Truly, the miracle of forgiveness finalizes the healing of ruptured cords of spiritual integrity.

## COMMITMENT TO INTEGRITY

Our personal integrity will be protected by prior commitments. Job secured his commitment to integrity before facing a challenge. He wrote:

"All the while my breath is in me, and the spirit of God is in my nostrils;

"My lips shall not speak wickedness, nor my tongue utter deceit. . . .

"Till I die I will not remove mine integrity from me."[17]

Job knew he would face his Maker one day in judgment. He recorded this hope: "Let me be weighed in an even balance, that God may know mine integrity."[18]

Shakespeare also penned a strong prior commitment to integrity through lines he gave to his character Tarquinius in the poem *Lucrece*. During a moment of mental weakness, Tarquinius contemplated the conquest of a woman in lust. He temporarily repaired that flaw in his own thinking when he declared:

What win I, if I gain the thing I seek?

A dream, a breath, a froth of fleeting joy.

Who buys a minute's mirth to wail a week?

Or sells eternity to get a toy?

For one sweet grape who will the vine destroy?[19]

"Pawning his honor to obtain his lust," however, Tarquinius rejected wisdom.[20] As a result, he lost his integrity, then his life.

Commitments to integrity are learned from parents. A proverb teaches that "the just man walketh in his integrity: his children are blessed after him."[21]

The Prophet Joseph Smith appreciated the integrity of his faithful brother, Hyrum. So did the Lord, who said: "Blessed is my servant Hyrum Smith; for I, the Lord, love him because of the integrity of his heart, and because he loveth that which is right before me."[22]

The Prophet Joseph added: "Blessed of the Lord is my brother Hyrum for the integrity of his heart; he shall be girt about with strength[;] truth and faithfulness shall be the strength of his loins. From generation to generation he shall be a shaft in the hand of his God."[23]

That prophecy has been fulfilled. Direct descendants of Hyrum Smith stand as strong leaders of the Church today. Likewise, the integrity we develop now will be a model for our own children. Generations yet unborn will be influenced by our integrity of heart.

### IDENTITY AND INTEGRITY

If my fondest wish could be granted, it would be that we could know who we really are, and that we know we come from premortal realms where we were numbered "among the noble and great ones who were chosen in the beginning to be rulers in the Church of God.

"Even before [we] were born, [we], with many others, received [our] first lessons in the world of spirits and were prepared to come forth in the due time of the Lord to labor in his vineyard for the salvation of the souls of men."[24]

Our precious identity deserves our precious integrity! We must guard it as the priceless prize it is.

I reiterate counsel the Prophet Joseph Smith gave his friends: "Seek to know God in your closets, call upon him in the fields. Follow the directions of the Book of Mormon, and pray over, and for your families, . . . and all things that you possess; ask the blessing of God upon all your labors, and everything that you engage in. Be virtuous and pure; be men [and women] of integrity and truth; keep the commandments of God; and then you will be able more perfectly to understand the difference between right and wrong—between the things of God and the things of men; and your path will be like that of the just, which shineth brighter and brighter unto the perfect day."[25]

God bless us to achieve that full measure of our creation—to maintain, to strengthen, and to cherish our integrity of heart.

NOTES

1. D&C 29:34.

2. D&C 88:36, 38.

3. D&C 88:47.

4. 2 Nephi 28:8–9.

5. *Deseret News Weekly,* 7 (25 November 1857), 300.

6. See Genesis 29:11–13.

7. See Romans 6:23.

8. Matthew 5:19.

9. Revelation 2:5.

10. Isaiah 35:3–4; see also D&C 81:5.

11. *Vital Quotations,* comp. Emerson Roy West (Salt Lake City: Bookcraft, 1968), 167.

12. Ether 12:37.

13. Ether 12:37; see also Ether 12:27; 2 Corinthians 12:9.

14. *Deseret News Semiweekly,* 2 (14 September 1867), 75.

15. D&C 101:4–5.

16. *Deseret News Semiweekly,* 2 (3 December 1867), 86.

17. Job 27:3–5.

18. Job 31:6.

19. *Lucrece,* Act 1, lines 211–15.

20. See *Lucrece,* Act 1, line 156.

21. Proverbs 20:7.

22. D&C 124:15.

23. *Teachings of the Prophet Joseph Smith,* 40.

24. D&C 138:55–56; see also Abraham 3:22.

25. *Teachings of the Prophet Joseph Smith,* 247.

# FUNDAMENTALS AND INITIATIVES

I see the proper balancing of two considerations—fundamentals and initiatives—as one of the great challenges of life.

Let us first turn our attention to the fundamentals.

## FUNDAMENTALS

I have learned that the wise physician asks himself at least two basic questions when confronted with any patient who is ill. Question number one: Will this illness subside with the passage of time, or will it become steadily more severe? For example, if a patient has a broken rib, it will get better with the passage of time. On the other hand, if a patient has a broken mitral valve in the heart, the patient will steadily deteriorate and die.

Question number two is considered if the answer to question number one is an ominous prognosis. If the illness is indeed steadily progressive, can that deteriorating course be changed by medical or surgical intervention? In the instance of a fractured mitral valve, the downhill progression can be reversed with surgical repair or placement of that broken valve.

The conscientious physician devotes much of his study to learn the natural laws that govern the area of his concern. We could say the same for the aerospace engineer or the jet pilot whose understanding of the physical laws of "foil" and "lift" is vitally important.

**Divine Law.** Let us mentally portray the first fundamental principle as a circle of *divine law.* Divine law is incontrovertible. It includes not only the laws of physics and physiology, but divine commandments as well. It pertains to things of eternal and ever-lasting worth, such as family, father, mother, children, ordinances, covenants, and doctrine. Divine law is the most basic of the fundamentals, obedience to which may begin the building of a life of greatness. Reference is made in the scriptures to this first fundamental:

"All kingdoms have a law given;

"And there are many kingdoms; for there is . . . no kingdom in which there is no space, either a greater or a lesser kingdom.

"And unto every kingdom is given a law; and unto every law there are certain bounds also and conditions."[1]

**Rules.** The second fundamental principle is also basic to success. It is the circle of *rules.* This ring includes the laws of man that can be made and also changed by human endeavor. In the Church, we are subject to rules written in the *General Handbook of Instructions.* Not only do we obey our own Church rules, but we also heed those of the society in which we live. We charge our members to be "subject to kings, presidents, rulers, and magistrates," and to obey, honor, and sustain the law.[2]

Government by law—both in word and practice—is the strength and bulwark of any democracy. No individual is to be above or below the law. This circle of *rules* must be added to the fundamentals upon which we build our lives.

**Policies.** The next fundamental principle is that of *policies.* Policies are established, for example, by governing boards and presidential bodies, who may also change those policies. In the

Church, we believe in continuing revelation to presiding leaders who have been given authority and responsibility. The men you sustain as prophets, seers, and revelators respond to inspiration from Him who said, "Whether by mine own voice or by the voice of my servants, it is the same."[3]

**Guidelines.** Next, consider the importance of *guidelines*. Guidelines can be written to assist those at work, at school, at home, or at church. I know a man who really understands guidelines. He assists the General Authorities by studying all proposals to purchase or improve real property for the Church. I asked him once how he was able to formulate so many important recommendations he must make to the Brethren. He simply replied, "I work within my guidelines."

If we examine these rings from another perspective, perhaps we can see what he meant. He establishes guidelines well within the circle of policies set by the Brethren. They, in turn, function within rules of the Church and civil government. And those rules are well within bounds set by divine law.

**Style.** Now let us discuss the final fundamental—that of *style*. This circle includes personality, determination, and spirit. A scripture uniquely applies to personal style:

"He that is compelled in all things, the same is a slothful and not a wise servant. . . .

"Men should be anxiously engaged in a good cause, and do many things of their own free will, and bring to pass much righteousness;

"For the power is in them, wherein they are agents unto themselves."[4]

As we crown this stack with the ring of *style,* note the importance of the central rod that is firmly attached to the basic ring of *divine law.* (See Figure 1.) This tie-rod may be likened to the scriptural term "the iron rod."[5]

*Figure 1.*

## Fundamentals

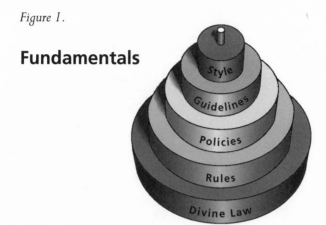

Variations in personal style should range within established guidelines, implemented policies, official rules, and divine law.

When properly stacked, these rings resemble a pyramid in shape. If our behavior is centered in Christ—and the iron rod attaches us firmly at any level of our activity to the fundamentals of God's commandments and things of eternal worth—then we won't so likely be tipped over by winds of adversity.

The heaviest weight in the pyramid is on the bottom. That gives great stability. In a way, it is similar to the heavy ballast in the bottom of an ocean liner, placed there so the ship won't be blown over in a storm.

Periodically we learn of individuals who either are not well anchored or are obsessed with a particular idea that extends beyond the limits imposed by guidelines, policies, rules, or even divine law. Such a style may be portrayed as eccentric. This is an unstable situation that leads to wobbly imbalance. (See Figure 2.)

*Figure 2.*

## Eccentric Style

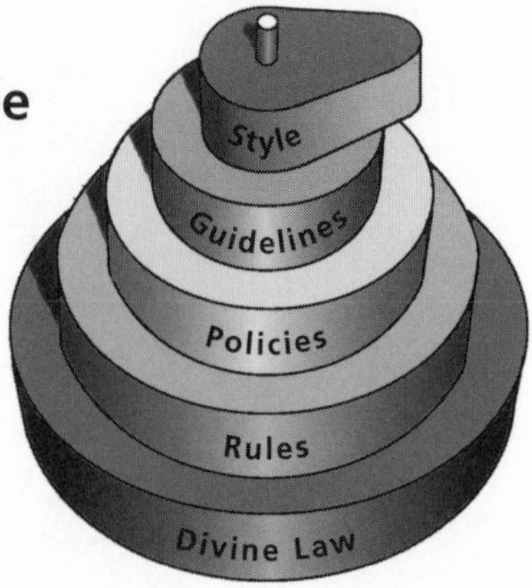

### INITIATIVE

Having considered the fundamentals, let us turn our attention now to individual initiative. This topic relates to one's freedom to act as a citizen in society or as a responsible member of the Church. The image of the cone of individual initiative takes the inverted shape of the pyramidal cone of fundamentals. It is shaped more like a top. (See Figure 3.)

As individuals, we have no latitude to break the commandments of God. They are absolutes for our conduct. "Thou shalt not commit adultery," for example, is an irrevocable commandment and part of *divine law.*

There is a little more room for initiative under the *rules* by which we live. Handbooks can be edited; new statutes can be passed; even a constitution can be amended.

New *policies* can be even more easily established—but only by those who formulated them in the first place.

*Guidelines* give even greater freedom for adaptation to particular circumstances.

The zone of greatest individual initiative is in the ring of *style.*

36

*Figure 3.*

# Individual Initiative

We previously referred to the word of the Lord that "he that is compelled in all things, the same is a slothful and not a wise servant."[6] So we are expected to exercise much individual initiative.

Inasmuch as this cone of individual initiative is to be put in motion, imagine rapidly rotating it to resemble a spinning top or a whirling gyroscope. A top spins well on a sturdy pivot-point. It also spins well only if there is no lopsided projection to deform its shape.

In our model, the laws of physics dictate that the forces generated by the spin provide lift in both outward and upward directions. (See Figure 4.)

To me, this teaches a lesson. If individual initiatives are free from abrasive burrs and well based on a firm foundation, there is great potential for personal spiritual growth.

The Lord said, "What manner of men ought ye to be? . . . Even as I am."[7] How can one's personal progress approach that of the Lord's hopes for us? It is by exercising individual initiative upward and outward, while remaining within the limits of the fundamental bounds and conditions we have discussed.

*Figure 4.*

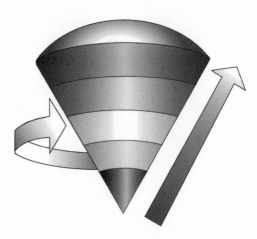

## APPLICATION OF THE THEORY

So much for the theory. This strategy can be applied to the lives of real people.

In the 3 March 1990 issue of the *Church News,* there was a report of the official recognition of the Church by the government in Czechoslovakia. A photograph showed Elder Hans B. Ringger and me meeting with Dr. Josef Hromadka, deputy prime minister of that country. The fourth person in that picture was Jiří Šnederfler, district president of the Church in Czechoslovakia. The accompanying account was truly historic! But another unpublished story preceded that story.

As General Authorities of the Church, we had been petitioning for official recognition in Czechoslovakia for a number of years. When Elder Ringger and I met with the minister of religious affairs of the country for the first time, we asked him what must be done in order to gain official recognition that would allow members of the Church in Czechoslovakia to meet in dignity and in full compliance with the law. He replied, "First, you will have to submit statutes indicating your religious beliefs. And they must be submitted not by you 'foreigners,' but by members of your Church here in Czechoslovakia. One of those members must be willing to meet with us and submit those statutes in person. Following that, we will consider your request."

Bear in mind that at this time, some citizens of Czechoslovakia were incarcerated in jail for expression of religious belief or dissident thought. (In fact, shortly before Vaclav Havel became the new president of the Czechoslovakian Republic, he was among those prisoners.) Not only that, but for nearly four decades, our faithful Latter-day Saints had met quietly only in their homes.

After our meeting with the minister of religious affairs, Elder Ringger and I conferred privately with our district president, Jiří Šnederfler, and his wife, Olga. We explained what was required. Then we asked him, "Are you willing to expose yourself as a member of The Church of Jesus Christ of Latter-day Saints? Are you willing to take the risk, knowing that it might mean jail or death if you were to identify yourself as the leader of the Church in this country?" We assured him that as his ecclesiastical authorities, we could not and would not make that request of him. We could only ask him to determine what his own conscience would allow him to do.

Bravely he replied, "Of course I will do it! I will reveal myself. I will meet with the magistrate. I will take the statutes to him personally. I will submit myself to his mercy." Then he concluded, "I will take whatever risk is necessary and even pay with my life, if needed, for the cause of the Lord and His Church because I know the gospel is true!" His wife gave her approval as tears of love moistened her eyes.

God bless Brother and Sister Šnederfler for their courage. They are the unsung heroes in the drama that made this significant announcement possible. Because of them, the Church has entered a new era of growth in the Czech Republic. A mission was reestablished there in July 1990 after an absence of forty years.

Brother and Sister Šnederfler are each noble examples of individual initiative balanced on fundamentals. They have been magnified and made great in the eyes of God and their fellowmen.

Valiant action occasionally entails risk. One's reputation— one's very life—may be put on the line. Modern scripture suggests that this may be required of each of us. In speaking of our day when the Lord would come to make up His jewels, He spoke of the trials to which His Saints may be subjected:

"They must needs be chastened and tried, even as Abraham, who was commanded to offer up his only son.

"For all those who will not endure chastening, but deny me, cannot be sanctified."[8]

In a way, every leader in the Church has to endure trials. Every stake president, bishop, elders quorum president, and teacher has similar and challenging opportunities for individual initiative. When balanced in motion and upon sound fundamental principles, deeds of greatness can result.

## THE SPIRIT OF THE LAW

It is one thing to become expert in the *letter* of the law. But even more challenging is the ability to master the *spirit* of the law. President Ezra Taft Benson often told us that the most important thing about our work in the Church is the Spirit.

A similar expression was uniquely voiced in 1990 by Dr. Hromadka, then deputy prime minister of the Republic of Czechoslovakia. We conversed with him about the challenges faced by a new government in a land where so much is needed. We asked if we, as members of The Church of Jesus Christ of

Latter-day Saints, could be of any help to his people. He knew that our Church is well recognized for its efforts in providing humanitarian relief throughout the world. We shall never forget his reply. He said, "We don't need material goods or technology. We need a new spirit. We need moral values. We need the Judeo-Christian ethic back in our curriculum. Please help us to make this a time of spiritual renewal for our nation!"

The new president of Czechoslovakia, Vaclav Havel, won the admiration of his audience when he addressed a joint session of the United States Congress. He did not hold an empty hat in hand. He asked only for spiritual assistance—not just for himself, but also for his neighbor.

This man who had been unjustly imprisoned for so long and could have felt unkindly toward his captors said, "I cannot hate; I will not hate." As he spoke to the combined assembly of the United States Congress, he made this impassioned plea for spiritual help:

"The worst thing is that we are living in a decayed moral environment. We have become morally ill, because we have become accustomed to saying one thing and thinking another. We have learned not to believe in anything, not to have consideration for one another and only to look after ourselves. Notions such as love, friendship, compassion, humility, and forgiveness have lost their depth and dimension, and for many of us they represent merely a psychological idiosyncrasy, or appear to be some kind of stray relic, something rather comical in the era of computers and space rockets."

What a marvelous message! President Havel's hopes for love, friendship, compassion, humility, and forgiveness hark right back to counsel given through the ages by living prophets of God. They have stressed the importance of practicing those principles broadly and especially within the walls of our own homes.

## BALANCE BETWEEN FUNDAMENTALS AND INITIATIVES

A society with no other scale than a legal one is not worthy of sons and daughters of God. Any morality based solely on the letter of the law falls short of the great potential of the human soul.

I plead for a proper balance between fundamentals and initiatives. Actions based on eternal principles enlarge the soul. Through such actions, in fact, we literally can become more like the Lord. We need not be boastful, but we can literally achieve the goal Jesus Christ expressed for us. "What manner of men ought ye to be?" He asked. Then He answered His own question: "Even as I am."[9] As we try to pattern our lives after the Savior's, we will be exhilarated, enlarged, ennobled, and magnified beyond our fondest dreams.

I testify that God lives, that Jesus is the Christ, that His restored church provides the pathway by which we can achieve balanced growth in this life and eternal glory in the life to come.

NOTES

1. D&C 88:36–38.
2. Articles of Faith 1:12.
3. D&C 1:38.
4. D&C 58:26–28.
5. See 1 Nephi 15:23–24.
6. D&C 58:26.
7. 3 Nephi 27:27.
8. D&C 101:4–5.
9. 3 Nephi 27:27.

# LISTEN TO LEARN

---

M any articles in Church literature have dealt with the important art of listening.[1] They support a proverb that teaches this vital lesson: "Hear counsel, and receive instruction, that thou mayest be wise."[2] Surely wisdom will come as we *listen to learn* from children, parents, partners, neighbors, Church leaders, and the Lord.

## CHILDREN

Parents and teachers, learn to listen, then listen to learn from children. A wise father once said, "I do a greater amount of good when I listen to my children than when I talk to them."[3]

When our youngest daughter was about four years of age, I came home from hospital duties quite late one evening. I found my dear wife to be very weary. I don't know why. She only had nine children underfoot all day. So I offered to get our four-year-old ready for bed. I began to give the orders: "Take off your clothes; hang them up; put on your pajamas; brush your teeth; say your prayers," and so on, commanding in a manner befitting a tough sergeant in the army. Suddenly she cocked her head to one side, looked at me with a wistful eye, and said, "Daddy, do you own me?"

She taught me an important lesson. I was using coercive methods on this sweet soul. To rule children by force is the technique of Satan, not of the Savior. No, we don't own our children. Our parental privilege is to love them, to lead them, and to let them go.

The time to listen is when someone needs to be heard. Children are naturally eager to share their experiences, which range from triumphs of delight to trials of distress. Are we as eager to listen? If they try to express their anguish, is it possible for us to listen openly to a shocking experience without going into a state of shock ourselves? Can we listen without interrupting and without making snap judgments that slam shut the door of dialogue? It can remain open with the soothing reassurance that we believe in them and understand their feelings. Adults should not pretend an experience did not happen just because they might wish otherwise.

Even silence can be misinterpreted. A story was written of "a little boy [who] looked up at his mother and said, 'Why are you mad at me?' She answered, 'I'm not angry at you. What makes you say that?' 'Well, your hands are on your hips, and you are not saying anything.'"[4]

Parents with teenage youth may find that time for listening is often less convenient but more important when young people feel lonely or troubled. And when they seem to deserve favor least, they may need it most.

Wise parents and teachers, listen to learn from children.

### PARENTS

Children of all ages, learn to listen, and listen to learn from parents. Spiritually or physically, it can be a matter of life and death.

Several years ago I was invited to give an important lecture at a medical school in New York City. The night before the lecture, Sister Nelson and I were invited to dinner at the home of our host professor. There he proudly introduced us to an honor medical student—his beautiful daughter.

Some weeks later, that professor telephoned me in an obvious state of grief. I asked, "What is the matter?"

"Remember our daughter whom you met at our home?"

"Of course," I replied. "I'll never forget such a stunning young lady."

Then her father sobbed and said, "Last night she was killed in an automobile accident!" Trying to gain composure, he continued: "She asked permission to go to a dance with a certain young man. I didn't have a good feeling about it. I told her so and asked her not to go. She asked, 'Why?' I simply told her that I was uneasy. She had always been an obedient daughter, but she said that if I could not give her a good reason to decline, she wanted to go. And so she did. At the dance, alcoholic beverages were served. Her escort drank a bit—we don't know how much. While returning home, he was driving too fast, missed a turn, and careened through a guardrail into a reservoir below. They were both submerged and taken to their death."

As I shared my feeling of sadness, he concluded: "My grief is made worse because I had the distinct feeling that trouble lay ahead. Why couldn't I have been more persuasive?"

This experience will not have been in vain if others can listen and learn from it. Children, honor your parents,[5] even when they cannot give a satisfactory explanation for their feelings. Please have faith in this scripture, which applies to all age groups: "Hear the instruction of thy father, and forsake not the law of thy mother."[6]

Parents have a divine duty to teach their children to love the

Lord.[7] Children have an equal obligation to "obey [their] parents in the Lord."[8]

Wise children, listen to learn from parents.

## PARTNERS

Husbands and wives, learn to listen, and listen to learn from one another. I was amused to read of an experience recorded by Elder F. Burton Howard in his biography of President Marion G. Romney:

"His good-humored love for Ida was manifested in many ways. He delighted in telling of her hearing loss. 'I once went to see a doctor about her hearing,' he would say. 'He asked me how bad it was, and I said I didn't know. He told me to go home and find out. The doctor instructed me to go into a far room and speak to her. Then I should move nearer and nearer until she does hear. Following the doctor's instructions, I spoke to her from the bedroom while she was in the kitchen—no answer. I moved nearer and spoke again—no answer. So I went right up to the door of the kitchen and said, "Ida, can you hear me?" She responded, "What is it, Marion? I've answered you three times." ' "[9]

Even with normal hearing, some couples seem not to listen to one another. Taking time to talk is essential to keep lines of communication intact. If marriage is a prime relationship in life, it deserves prime time! Yet less important appointments are often given priority, leaving only leftover moments for listening to precious partners.

Keeping the garden of marriage well cultivated and free from weeds of neglect requires the time and commitment of love. It is not only a pleasant privilege, it is a scriptural requirement with promise of eternal glory.[10]

Wise partners, listen to learn from one another.

## NEIGHBORS

Learn to listen, and listen to learn from neighbors. Repeatedly the Lord has said, "Thou shalt love thy neighbour."[11] Opportunities to listen to those of diverse religious or political persuasion can promote tolerance and learning. And a good listener will listen to a person's sentiments as well.

I learned much from Brother David M. Kennedy as we met with many dignitaries in nations abroad. When one of them spoke, Brother Kennedy not only looked eye to eye and listened with real intent, but he even removed his reading glasses, as if to show that he wanted nothing in the way of his total concentration.

The wise listen to learn from neighbors.

## CHURCH LEADERS

Members, learn to listen, and listen to learn from Church leaders. Faithful members love the Savior and honor His servants, having faith in the Lord's declaration that "whether by mine own voice or by the voice of my servants, it is the same."[12]

One day in Italy I met a wonderful priesthood leader and his wife. In him I saw a man with great potential. But my language was foreign to them. Through an interpreter, I challenged them to study the English language. They listened obediently and studied diligently. Six years later, ably sustained by his wife, Carolina, Vincenzo Conforte was faithfully serving his *second* assignment as a mission president, interviewing missionaries well in Italian or in English.

President Ezra Taft Benson proclaimed the importance of studying the Book of Mormon. People throughout the earth are being blessed as they follow this and other counsel given by latter-day prophets.

Gratefully we thank God for a prophet to guide us in these latter days. But many turn a deaf ear to the teachings of the living prophets, oblivious to their prophetic position. They do so at great risk, for scriptures contain this warning:

"A prophet shall the Lord your God raise up unto you . . . ; him shall ye hear in all things whatsoever he shall say unto you. . . .

"Every soul, which will not hear that prophet, shall be destroyed from among the people."[13]

President J. Reuben Clark, Jr., said, "We do not lack a prophet; what we lack is a listening ear."[14] Words of the Lord are taught by His disciples.[15] Wise members listen to learn from Church leaders.

## THE LORD

Above all, God's children should learn to listen, then listen to learn from the Lord. On several sacred occasions in the world's history, our Heavenly Father has personally appeared to introduce His divine Son with a specific charge to "*hear* him."[16]

Jesus taught this first and great commandment: "Thou shalt love the Lord thy God with all thy heart, and with all thy soul, and with all thy mind."[17]

Scriptures recorded in all dispensations teach that we show our *love* of God as we *hearken* to His commandments and *obey* them.[18] These actions are closely connected. In fact, the Hebrew language of the Old Testament in most instances uses the same term for both *hearkening* (to the Lord) and *obedience* (to His word).[19]

In addition to hearing the word of the Lord obediently, we manifest our love for God through prayer. And listening is an essential part of prayer. Answers from the Lord come ever so quietly. Hence He has counseled us to "be still and know that I am God."[20]

48

President Spencer W. Kimball said, "It would not hurt us . . . if we paused at the end of our prayers to do some intense listening—even for a moment or two—always praying, as the Savior did, 'not my will, but thine, be done' (Luke 22:42)."[21]

In a world scarred by scourges of tyranny and war, many of its inhabitants earnestly pray for inner peace. For example, not long ago a beautiful young mother named Svetlana developed an intense desire to obtain a Bible. But in her city of Leningrad (now St. Petersburg), a Bible was very rare and expensive. Frequently and fervently she prayed for a Bible. Ultimately, she and her husband were impressed to travel with their small child to Helsinki, Finland, with that hope in mind. There one day while walking in a park, she stumbled across an object buried under the cover of autumn leaves. She picked it up and found it to be a Bible written in the Russian language!

Excitedly she recounted the story of this great discovery to another mother who was also in the park with her youngster. The second mother rejoiced with Svetlana and added, "Would you like to have *another* book about Jesus Christ?" Svetlana, of course, answered in the affirmative. The other mother provided Svetlana with a copy of a Russian-language edition of the Book of Mormon and invited the family to church. She eagerly embraced the teachings of the missionaries and shortly thereafter joined The Church of Jesus Christ of Latter-day Saints. Then they returned to their home, where they helped pioneer the work in the Leningrad Branch of the Church.[22]

Her experience typifies this promise of the Savior to those who seek Him: "Thus saith the Lord God: I will give unto the children of men line upon line, precept upon precept, here a little and there a little; and blessed are those who *hearken* unto my precepts, and *lend an ear* unto my counsel, for they shall learn wisdom; for unto him that receiveth I will give more."[23]

While stressing the importance of listening well, I am mindful of those who cannot hear. Many labeled as deaf have received the Spirit "by the hearing of faith."[24] The example of Rachel Ivins Grant is inspiring to me. She never complained about her own deafness. Though most women in their seventies would be completely worn out while rearing six growing children of another mother, she undertook that task. Rachel's deafness seemed to save her from the wear and tear of noise. Sometimes, when two were arguing, Rachel would burst out laughing. She said they had no idea how funny it was to see their angry faces and hear none of their words.

Before her son, Heber J. Grant, became the seventh President of the Church, she declared, "Of course the greatest trial I have is that I cannot hear, but I have so many blessings I cannot complain, but if we only will live so that we may receive the instructions of God, there is nothing we are called to pass through but will be for our good."[25]

The Redeemer loves such faithful souls: "For the eyes of the Lord are over the righteous, and his ears are open unto their prayers."[26]

They qualify for this prophetic promise: "Before they call, I [the Lord] will answer; and while they are yet speaking, I will hear."[27]

To all of God's children, either able to hear or deaf to mortal sound, He offers this reward: "Incline your ear, and come unto me: hear, and your soul shall live."[28]

Your soul will be blessed as you learn to listen, then listen to learn from children, parents, partners, neighbors, and Church leaders, all of which will heighten capacity to hear counsel from on high.

Carefully listen to learn from the Lord through the still small voice—the Holy Spirit—which leads to truth.[29] Listen to learn by studying scriptures that record His holy mind and will.[30] Listen to learn in prayer, for He will answer the humble who truly seek Him.[31]

The wise listen to learn from the Lord. I testify of Him and certify that as we "hearken and . . . hear the voice of the Lord," we will be blessed, "for the hour of his coming is nigh."[32]

NOTES

1. Examples include:

Marvin J. Ashton, "Family Communications," *New Era,* October 1978, 7–9.

Lynne Baker, "Please Take Time to Listen!" *Improvement Era,* November 1968, 110–13.

Marilyn A. Bullock, "Listening to My Two-Year-Old," *Ensign,* January 1983, 70.

Henry B. Eyring, "Listen Together," in *1988–89 Devotional and Fireside Speeches* (Provo, Utah: Brigham Young University, 1989), 11–21.

Winnifred C. Jardine, "Listen with All of You," *Ensign,* February 1974, 51.

Larry K. Langlois, "When Couples Don't Listen to Each Other," *Ensign,* September 1989, 16–19.

Boyd K. Packer, "Prayers and Answers," *Ensign,* November 1979, 19–21.

H. Burke Peterson, "Preparing the Heart," *Ensign,* May 1990, 83–84.

Viewpoint Editorial, "Giving with Your Ears," *Church News,* 13 January 1985, 16.

Youth Authors, "Parents, Are You Listening?" *Ensign,* February 1971, 54–57.

2. Proverbs 19:20; see also Proverbs 8:32–33; Jacob 6:12.

3. George D. Durrant, "Take Time to Talk," *Ensign,* April 1973, 24; see also James 1:19.

4. Florence B. Pinnock, "Let's Listen," *Improvement Era,* October 1964, 872–73.

5. See Exodus 20:12; Deuteronomy 5:16; Matthew 15:4; 19:19; Mark 7:10; 10:19; Luke 18:20; Ephesians 6:2; 1 Nephi 17:55; Mosiah 13:20.

6. Proverbs 1:8.

7. See Leviticus 10:11; Deuteronomy 4:10; 6:7; 11:19; Mosiah 1:4; D&C 68:25, 28; Moses 6:57–58.

8. Ephesians 6:1; see also Colossians 3:20.

9. F. Burton Howard, *Marion G. Romney: His Life and Faith* (Salt Lake City: Bookcraft, 1988), 144–45.

10. See Ephesians 5:25, 33; Colossians 3:19; 1 Peter 3:1; Jacob 3:7; D&C 132:19.

11. Leviticus 19:18; Matthew 19:19; see also Matthew 22:39; Mark 12:31, 33; Luke 10:27; Romans 13:9; Galatians 5:14; James 2:8; Mosiah 23:15; D&C 59:6.

12. D&C 1:38.

13. Acts 3:22–23; see also Jeremiah 5:21; D&C 1:14.

14. J. Reuben Clark, Jr., "Not a Prophet—but a Listening Ear," *Improvement Era,* November 1948, 685.

15. See D&C 1:4.

16. See Matthew 17:5; Mark 9:7; Luke 9:35; 3 Ne. 11:7; JS—H 1:17; emphasis added.

17. Matthew 22:37.

18. See Exodus 20:6; Deuteronomy 5:10; 7:9; 11:1; 30:16; Joshua 22:5; Nehemiah 1:5; Daniel 9:4; John 14:15; 15:10; 1 John 5:2–3; 2 John 1:6; Mosiah 13:14; D&C 42:2; 46:9; 124:87.

19. That term is שָׁמַע (shâma‘), which means "to hear intelligently." The term was used hundreds of times in the Hebrew Old Testament, as Israel was counseled to *hearken* to the word of the Lord and *obey* it.

Different terms were used in some instances in the Hebrew text whenever reference was made to hearing or responding *without* implied obedience. Examples:

• "They have ears, but they *hear* not" (Psalm 135:17; see also 140:6; emphasis added). Hebrew: אָזַן ('âzan), to give ear—to listen.

• "I will *hear,* saith the Lord, I will *hear* the heavens, and they shall *hear* the earth" (Hosea 2:21; emphasis added). Hebrew: עָנָה ('ânâh), to pay attention—to answer.

52

• "Lift up thy voice, O daughter . . . : cause it to be *heard*" (Isaiah 10:30; emphasis added; see also Psalm 10:17). Hebrew: קָשַׁב (qâshav), to give heed.

Still different terms were employed in the Old Testament when referring to obedience *not* to Deity but to other people. Examples:

• "The eye that mocketh at his father, and despiseth to *obey* his mother" (Proverbs 30:17; emphasis added). Hebrew: יְקָהָה (yiqqâhâh), obedience, to obey.

• "The children of Ammon shall *obey* them" (Isaiah 11:14; emphasis added). Hebrew: מִשְׁמַעַת (mishma'ath), audience—obedience.

That link between *listening* and *obedience* is found not only in Hebrew, but also in Latin and Greek. The word *obey* comes from two Latin roots: the prefix *ob* ("to" or "toward") and the root *audiō, audīre* ("to hear" or "to listen"). This root occurs in words such as *audio, audience,* and *auditorium.* Literally, then, the word *obey* means "to hear or to listen *toward,*" that is, "to comply."

The word for *obey* in Greek, ὑπακούω (hupakouō), literally means "listen under," from *hypo* ("under") as in *hypo-dermic,* also "in subjection or subordination," and the root *akouō* ("hear, listen") as in *acoustics.* In New Testament times, its use was gradually broadened to less sacred realms, including expressions such as "children, obey your parents" (Ephesians 6:1; Col. 3:20), "wives, [obey] husbands" (1 Peter 3:1), and "servants, obey . . . masters" (Colossians 3:22), and so on.

A parallel pattern is found in the Book of Mormon. Use of terms such as *listen, hear,* and *hearken,* written at the time of the Old Testament, generally carried the same implication of obedience to Deity. Those terms in Book of Mormon scriptures written *after* the earthly advent of Christ were also broadened to include the more familiar usage, as in the language of the New Testament.

20. D&C 101:16.

21. Spencer W. Kimball, "We Need a Listening Ear," *Ensign,* November 1979, 4–5.

22. Steven R. Mecham, president of the Finland Helsinki Mission, personal communication to the author, 26 April 1990. Svetlana's last name is Artemova. The name of the other mother is Raija Kemppainen, wife of Jussi Kemppainen, who at that time was president of the Baltic District of that mission.

23. 2 Nephi 28:30; emphasis added. See also D&C 29:7.

24. Galatians 3:2. For example, see Anne C. Bradshaw, "Listen with Your Heart," *New Era,* March 1989, 28–31.

25. *Woman's Exponent* (1 and 15 December 1902), 52. Earlier, at age 67, she wrote, "I look for the time when I will be able to hear by the power of God" (Ibid., 15 August 1888, 46).

26. 1 Peter 3:12.

27. Isaiah 65:24.

28. Isaiah 55:3; see also Mosiah 2:9; Alma 5:41; 36:3; 3 Nephi 23:5.

29. See 1 King 19:12; 1 Nephi 17:45; D&C 85:6.

30. See John 5:39; Alma 14:1; 33:2.

31. See Mosiah 9:18; 23:10; Alma 9:26; D&C 19:23; 112:10; Abraham 2:19; Joseph Smith—History, footnote, paragraph 5, 59.

32. D&C 133:16–17.

# THE CANKER OF CONTENTION

M y esteemed colleague Elder Carlos E. Asay and I once stood atop Mount Nebo, where Moses once stood.[1] We saw what he saw. In the distance to our right was the Sea of Galilee. The River Jordan flowed from there to the Dead Sea on our left. Ahead was the promised land into which Joshua led the Israelite faithful so long ago.

Later we were permitted to do what Moses could not. We were escorted from the Hashemite kingdom of Jordan to its western border with Israel. From there, we and our associates walked over the Allenby Bridge. We felt the tension as armed soldiers nearby guarded both sides of the international boundary.

After safely enduring this experience, I thought of the irony of it all. Here in the land made holy by the Prince of Peace, contention has existed almost continuously from that day to this.

Prior to His ascension from the Holy Land, the Savior pronounced a unique blessing: "Peace I leave with you, my peace I give unto you: not as the world giveth, give I unto you."[2]

His peace is not necessarily political; His peace is personal. But that spirit of inner peace is driven away by contention. Contention does not usually begin as strife between countries. More often, it starts with an individual, for we can contend within ourselves over simple matters of right and wrong. From there, contention can infect neighbors and nations like a spreading sore.

As we dread any disease that undermines the health of the body, so should we deplore contention, which is a corroding canker of the spirit. I appreciate the counsel of Abraham Lincoln, who said:

"Quarrel not at all. No man resolved to make the most of himself can spare time for personal contention. . . . Better give your path to a dog than be bitten by him."[3]

President Ezra Taft Benson described contention as "another face of pride."[4]

My concern is that contention is becoming accepted as a way of life. From what we see and hear in the media, the classroom, and the workplace, all are now infected to some degree with contention. How easy it is, yet how wrong it is, to allow habits of contention to pervade matters of spiritual significance, because contention is forbidden by divine decree:

"The Lord God hath commanded that men should not murder; that they should not lie; that they should not steal; that they should not take the name of the Lord their God in vain; that they should not envy; that they should not have malice; that they should not contend one with another."[5]

## CREATOR OF CONTENTION

To understand why the Lord has commanded us not to "contend one with another," we must know the true source of contention. A Book of Mormon prophet revealed this important knowledge even before the birth of Christ:

"Satan did stir them up to do iniquity continually; yea, he did go about spreading rumors and contentions upon all the face of the land, that he might harden the hearts of the people against that which was good and against that which should come."[6]

When Christ did come to the Nephites, He confirmed that prophecy:

"He that hath the spirit of contention is not of me [saith the Lord], but is of the devil, who is the father of contention, and he stirreth up the hearts of men to contend with anger, one with another.

"Behold, this is not my doctrine, to stir up the hearts of men with anger, one against another; but this is my doctrine, that such things should be done away."[7]

## ORIGIN OF CONTENTION

Contention existed before the earth was formed. When God's plan for creation and mortal life on the earth was first announced, sons and daughters of God shouted for joy. The plan was dependent on man's agency, his subsequent fall from the presence of God, and the merciful provision of a Savior to redeem mankind. Scriptures reveal that Lucifer sought vigorously to *amend* the plan by destroying the agency of man. Satan's cunning motive was unmasked in his statement:

"Behold, here am I, send me, I will be thy son, and I will redeem all mankind, that one soul shall not be lost, and surely I will do it; wherefore give me thine honor."[8]

Satan's selfish efforts to alter the plan of God resulted in great contention in heaven. The Prophet Joseph Smith explained:

"Jesus said there would be certain souls that would not be saved; and the devil said he could save them all, and laid his plans before the grand council, who gave their vote in favor of Jesus Christ. So the devil rose up in rebellion against God, and was cast down."[9]

57

This war in heaven was not a war of bloodshed. It was a war of conflicting ideas—the beginning of contention.

Scriptures repeatedly warn that the father of contention opposes the plan of our Heavenly Father. Satan's method relies on the infectious canker of contention. Satan's motive: to gain personal acclaim even over God Himself.

## TARGETS OF THE ADVERSARY

The work of the adversary may be likened to loading guns in opposition to the work of God. Salvos containing germs of contention are aimed and fired at strategic targets essential to that holy work. These vital targets include—in addition to the individual—the family, leaders of the Church, and divine doctrine.

## THE FAMILY

The family has been under attack ever since Satan first taunted Adam and Eve.[10] So today, each must guard against the hazard of contention in the family. It usually begins innocently. Years ago when our daughters were little girls who wanted to be big girls, the style of the day was to wear multiple petticoats. A little contention could have crept in as the girls soon learned that the one to get dressed first was the one best dressed.

In a large family of boys, those with the longest reach were the best fed. In order to avoid obvious contention, they adopted a rule that required them at mealtime to leave at least one foot on the floor.

The home is the great laboratory of learning and love. Here parents help children overcome these natural tendencies to be selfish. In rearing our own family, Sister Nelson and I have been very grateful for this counsel from the Book of Mormon:

"Ye will not suffer your children that they go hungry, or

naked; neither will ye suffer that they transgress the laws of God, and fight and quarrel one with another, . . .

"But ye will teach them to walk in the ways of truth and soberness; ye will teach them to love one another, and to serve one another."[11]

And I might add, please be patient while children learn those lessons.

Parents should be partners to cherish and protect one another, knowing that the aim of the adversary is to destroy the integrity of the family.

## LEADERS OF THE CHURCH

Leaders of the Church are targets for attack by those who stir contention. This is true even though not a single leader has called himself or herself to a position of responsibility. Each General Authority, for instance, chose another path to pursue as his life's occupation. But the reality is, as with Peter or Paul, each was surely "called of God, by prophecy, and by the laying on of hands by those who are in authority."[12] With that call comes the commitment to emulate the patterns of the Prince of Peace.

That goal is shared by worthy servants of the Master, who would not speak ill of the Lord's anointed nor provoke contention over teachings declared by ancient or living prophets.

Certainly no faithful follower of God would promote any cause even remotely related to religion if rooted in controversy, because contention is not of the Lord.

Surely a stalwart would not lend his or her good name to periodicals, programs, or forums that feature offenders who do sow "discord among brethren."[13]

Such agitators unfortunately fulfill long-foretold prophecy: they "take counsel together, against the Lord, and against his anointed."[14]

59

Yet, mercifully, the anointed pray for those who attack them, knowing the sad fate prophesied for their attackers.[15]

Throughout the world, Saints of the Lord follow Him *and* His anointed leaders. They have learned that the path of dissent leads to real dangers. The Book of Mormon carries this warning:

"Now these dissenters, having the same instruction and the same information . . . , having been instructed in the same knowledge of the Lord, nevertheless, it is strange to relate, not long after their dissensions they became more hardened and impenitent, and more wild, wicked and ferocious . . . ; giving way to indolence, and all manner of lasciviousness; yea, entirely forgetting the Lord their God."[16]

How divisive is the force of dissension! Small acts can lead to such great consequences. Regardless of position or situation, no one can safely assume immunity to contention's terrible toll.

Thomas B. Marsh, once one of the Twelve, left the Church. His spiritual slide to apostasy started because his wife and another woman had quarreled over a little cream! After an absence from the Church of nearly nineteen years, he came back. To a congregation of Saints, he then said:

"If there are any among this people who should ever apostatize and do as I have done, prepare your backs for a good whipping, if you are such as the Lord loves. But if you will take my advice, you will stand by the authorities."[17]

Of course the authorities are human. But to them God has entrusted the keys to His divine work. And He holds us accountable for our responses to the teachings of His servants. These are the words of the Lord:

"If my people will hearken unto my voice, and unto the voice of my servants whom I have appointed to lead my people, behold, verily I say unto you, they shall not be moved out of their place.

"But if they will not hearken to my voice, nor unto the voice of these men whom I have appointed, they shall not be blest."[18]

## DIVINE DOCTRINE

Divine doctrine of the Church is the prime target of attack by the spiritually contentious. Well do I remember a friend who would routinely sow seeds of contention in Church classes. His assaults would invariably be preceded by this predictable comment: "Let me play the role of devil's advocate." Recently he passed away. One day he will stand before the Lord in judgment. Then, I wonder, will my friend's predictable comment again be repeated?

Such contentious spirits are not new. In an epistle to Timothy, the Apostle Paul gave this warning, "that the name of God and his doctrine be not blasphemed."[19]

"If any man teach otherwise, and consent not to wholesome words, even the words of our Lord Jesus Christ, and to [his] doctrine, . . . doting about questions and strifes of words, . . . supposing that gain is godliness: from such withdraw thyself."[20]

Dissecting doctrine in a controversial way in order to draw attention to oneself is not pleasing to the Lord. He declared:

"Bring to light the true points of my doctrine, yea, and the only doctrine which is in me.

"And this I do that I may establish my gospel, that there may not be so much contention; yea, Satan doth stir up the hearts of the people to contention concerning the points of my doctrine; and in these things they do err, for they do wrest the scriptures and do not understand them."[21]

Contention fosters disunity. The Book of Mormon teaches the better way:

"Alma, having authority from God, . . . commanded them that there should be no contention one with another, but that

61

they should look forward with one eye, having one faith and one baptism, having their hearts knit together in unity and in love one towards another."[22]

## STEPS TO SUPPLANT CONTENTION

What can we do to combat this canker of contention? What steps may each of us take to supplant the spirit of contention with a spirit of personal peace?

To begin, show compassionate concern for others. Control the tongue, the pen, and the word processor. Whenever tempted to dispute, remember this proverb: "He that is void of wisdom despiseth his neighbour: but a man of understanding holdeth his peace."[23]

Bridle the passion to speak or write contentiously for personal gain or glory. The Apostle Paul thus counseled the Philippians, "Let nothing be done through strife or vainglory; but in lowliness of mind let each esteem other better than themselves."[24]

Such high mutual regard would then let us respectfully disagree without being disagreeable.

But the ultimate step lies beyond beginning control of expression. Personal peace is reached when one, in humble submissiveness, truly loves God. Heed carefully this scripture:

"There was no contention in the land, *because of* the love of God which did dwell in the hearts of the people."[25]

Thus, love of God should be our aim. It is the first commandment—the foundation of faith. As we develop love of God and Christ, love of family and neighbor will naturally follow. Then will we eagerly emulate Jesus. He healed. He comforted. He taught, "Blessed are the peacemakers: for they shall be called the children of God."[26]

Through love of God, the pain caused by the fiery canker of

contention will be extinguished from the soul. This healing begins with a personal vow: "Let there be peace on earth, and let it begin with me."[27] This commitment will then spread to family and friends and will bring peace to neighborhoods and nations.

Shun contention. Seek godliness. Be enlightened by eternal truth. Be like-minded with the Lord in love and united with Him in faith. Then shall "the peace of God, which passeth all understanding"[28] be yours, to bless you and your posterity through generations yet to come.

NOTES

1. See Deuteronomy 34:1–4.

2. John 14:27.

3. Letter to J. M. Cutts, 26 October 1863, in *Concise Lincoln Dictionary of Thoughts and Statements,* comp. and arr. Ralph B. Winn (New York: Philosophical Library, 1959), 107.

4. "Beware of Pride," *Ensign,* May 1989, 6.

5. 2 Nephi 26:32.

6. Helaman 16:22.

7. 3 Nephi 11:29–30.

8. Moses 4:1.

9. *Teachings of the Prophet Joseph Smith,* 357.

10. See Genesis 3; Moses 4.

11. Mosiah 4:14–15.

12. Articles of Faith 1:5.

13. Proverbs 6:19; see also 6:14.

14. Psalm 2:2.

15. See D&C 121:16–22.

16. Alma 47:36.

17. In *Journal of Discourses,* 5:206; see also Gordon B. Hinckley, in *Ensign,* May 1984, 81–83.

18. D&C 124:45–46.

19. 1 Timothy 6:1.

20. 1 Timothy 6:3–5; see also Isaiah 29:21; 2 Nephi 27:32; D&C 19:30; 38:41; 60:14.

21. D&C 10:62–63.

22. Mosiah 18:18, 21; see also 23:15.

23. Proverbs 11:12; see also 17:28.

24. Philippians 2:3.

25. 4 Nephi 1:15; emphasis added. See also 4 Nephi 1:2.

26. Matthew 5:9; see also 3 Nephi 12:9.

27. "Let There Be Peace on Earth," Sy Miller and Jill Jackson, © JanLee Music, Beverly Hills, Calif., 1972.

28. Philippians 4:7.

# "Teach Us Tolerance and Love"

---

Tolerance is a virtue much needed in our turbulent world. In discussing this topic, we must recognize at the outset that there is a difference between *tolerance* and *tolerate*. Your gracious tolerance for an individual does not grant him or her license to do wrong, nor does your tolerance obligate you to tolerate his or her misdeed. That distinction is fundamental to an understanding of this vital virtue.

I attended a "laboratory of tolerance" some years ago when I had the privilege of participating in the Parliament of the World's Religions. There I conversed with good men and women representing many religious groups. Again I sensed the advantages of ethnic and cultural diversity and reflected once more on the importance of religious freedom and tolerance.

I marvel at the inspiration of the Prophet Joseph Smith when he penned the eleventh article of faith: "We claim the privilege of worshiping Almighty God according to the dictates of our own conscience, and allow all men the same privilege, let them worship how, where, or what they may."

That noble expression of religious tolerance is particularly poignant in light of the Prophet's personal persecution. On one occasion he wrote, "I am at this time persecuted the worst of any man on the earth, as well as this people, . . . all our sacred rights are trampled under the feet of the mob."[1]

Joseph Smith endured incessant persecution and finally heartless martyrdom—at the hands of the intolerant. His brutal fate stands as a stark reminder that we must never be guilty of *any* sin sown by the seed of intolerance.

## THE TWO GREAT COMMANDMENTS TO LOVE

Revealed to that revered prophet was the fulness of the gospel. He was tutored by the resurrected Christ, whom Joseph adored. He taught doctrines declared by the Lord, including these He gave in response to the question of an exacting lawyer:

"Master, which is the great commandment in the law?

"Jesus said unto him, Thou shalt love the Lord thy God with all thy heart, and with all thy soul, and with all thy mind.

"This is the first and great commandment.

"And the second is like unto it, Thou shalt love thy neighbour as thyself.

"On these two commandments hang all the law and the prophets."[2]

Hence, our highest priorities in life are to love God and to love our neighbors. That broadly includes neighbors in our own family, our community, our nation, and our world. Obedience to the second commandment facilitates obedience to the first commandment. "When ye are in the service of your fellow beings ye are only in the service of your God."[3]

## PARENTAL LOVE

That concept is easy for mothers and fathers to understand. Parental love includes gratitude for service extended to any of their children, especially in their time of need.

66

I was amused recently when one of our grown children confided that she had always thought that she was her daddy's favorite daughter. She was surprised to discover later that each of her eight sisters harbored that same feeling. Only when they had become mothers themselves did they realize that parents hardly have favorites. (Incidentally, our only son never had to wonder who was our favorite son.)

Our Father in Heaven loves all of His children, too. Peter taught that "God is no respecter of persons:

"But in every nation he that feareth him, and worketh righteousness, is accepted with him."[4]

Yet His children can be so intolerant with one another. Neighboring factions, whether they be identified as groups or gangs, schools or states, counties or countries, often develop animosity. Such tendencies make me wonder: Cannot boundary lines exist without becoming battle lines? Could not people unite in waging war against the evils that beset mankind instead of waging war on each other? Sadly, answers to these questions are often no. Through the years, discrimination based on ethnic or religious identity has led to senseless slaughter, vicious pogroms, and countless acts of cruelty. The face of history is pocked by the ugly scars of intolerance.

How different our world would be if all parents would apply this inspired instruction from the Book of Mormon: "Ye will not suffer your children . . . that they transgress the laws of God, and fight and quarrel one with another. . . .

"But ye will teach them to walk in the ways of truth and soberness; ye will teach them to love one another, and to serve one another."[5]

If such training occurred, children and parents around this globe would join in singing, "Fill our hearts with sweet forgiving; Teach us tolerance and love."[6] Men and women would respect their neighbors and the beliefs held sacred by them. No longer would ethnic jokes and cultural slurs be acceptable. The tongue of the tolerant speaks no guile.

## INDEPENDENCE AND COOPERATION

While we strive for the virtue of tolerance, other commendable qualities need not be lost. Tolerance does not require the surrender of noble purpose or of individual identity. The Lord gave instruction to leaders of His restored church to establish and maintain institutional integrity—"that the church may stand independent."[7]

Meanwhile, its members are encouraged to join with like-minded citizens in doing good.[8] We are grateful for the many examples of heroic service rendered in times of earthquakes, floods, hurricanes, or other disasters. Such cooperative efforts to help neighbors in distress transcend any barriers posed by religion, race, or culture. Those good deeds are latter-day love in action!

Humanitarian relief rendered by members of this Church is extensive, multinational, and generally unpublicized. Even so, there are doubtless many who wonder why we don't do more to assist the innumerable worthy causes to which our hearts respond.

Of course we are concerned with the need for ambulances in the valley below. But at the same time, we cannot ignore the greater need for protective guardrails on the cliffs above. Limited resources needed for the accomplishment of the higher work cannot be depleted in rescue efforts that provide only temporary relief.

The biblical prophet Nehemiah must have felt that same commitment to his important calling. When he was asked to divert attention away from his primary purpose, he replied: "I am doing a great work, so that I cannot come down: why should the work cease, whilst I leave it, and come down to you?"[9]

Fortunately, we in the Church rarely have to make such a decision. We consider love of neighbor an integral part of our mission. And while we serve one another, we continue to build a spiritual house of refuge on the cliffs above. Such a sanctuary becomes a blessing for all mankind. We are but the builders; the architect is almighty God.

## MISSIONARY RESPONSIBILITIES

Latter-day Saints throughout the world work side by side with others—regardless of race, color, or creed—hoping to be good examples worthy of emulation. The Savior said, "I give unto you a commandment, that every man, both elder, priest, teacher, and also member, . . . prepare and accomplish the things which I have commanded.

"And let your preaching be the warning voice, every man to his neighbor, in mildness and in meekness."[10]

This we are to do with tolerance. While in Moscow in June 1991, in that spirit of preparation and with sincere respect for leaders of other religious denominations, Elder Dallin H. Oaks and I had the privilege of meeting with the presiding official of the Russian Orthodox Church. We were accompanied by Elder Hans B. Ringger and the mission president, Gary L. Browning. Patriarch Aleksei was most gracious in sharing a memorable hour with us. We perceived the great difficulties endured for so many years by this kind man and his fellow believers. We thanked him for his perseverance and for his faith. Then we assured him of our good intentions and of the importance of the message that missionaries of The Church of Jesus Christ of Latter-day Saints would be teaching among his countrymen. We affirmed that ours is a global Church and that we honor and obey the laws of each land in which we labor.[11]

To those with an interest in the fulness of the restored gospel—regardless of nationality or religious background—we say as did Elder Bruce R. McConkie: "Keep all the truth and all the good that you have. Do not abandon any sound or proper principle. Do not forsake any standard of the past which is good, righteous, and true. Every truth found in every church in all the world we believe. But we also say this to all men—Come and take the added light and truth that God has restored in our day. The more truth we have, the greater is our joy here and now; the more truth we receive, the greater is our reward in eternity. This is our invitation to men [and women] of good will everywhere."[12]

Each of you with a testimony of the truth of the restored gospel has opportunity to share that precious gift. The Lord expects you to "be ready always to give an answer to every man that asketh you a reason of the hope that is in you with meekness."[13]

## BAPTISM TRANSCENDS BACKGROUND

On every continent and across isles of the sea, the faithful are being gathered into The Church of Jesus Christ of Latter-day Saints. Differences in cultural background, language, gender, and facial features fade into insignificance as members lose themselves in service to their beloved Savior. Paul's declaration is being fulfilled: "As many of you as have been baptized into Christ have put on Christ.

"There is neither Jew nor Greek, there is neither bond nor free, there is neither male nor female: for ye are all one in Christ Jesus."[14]

Only the comprehension of the true Fatherhood of God can bring full appreciation of the true brotherhood of man. That

70

understanding inspires desire to build bridges of cooperation instead of walls of segregation.

Our Creator decreed "that there should be no contention one with another, but that they should look forward with one eye, having one faith and one baptism, having their hearts knit together in unity and in love one towards another."[15]

Intolerance seeds contention; tolerance supersedes contention. Tolerance is the key that opens the door to mutual understanding and love.

## RISKS OF BOUNDLESS TOLERANCE

Now may I offer an important note of caution. An erroneous assumption could be made that if a little of something is good, a lot must be better. Not so! Overdoses of needed medication can be toxic. Boundless mercy could oppose justice. So tolerance, without limit, could lead to spineless permissiveness.

The Lord drew boundary lines to define acceptable limits of tolerance. Danger rises when those divine limits are disobeyed. Just as parents teach little children not to run and play in the street, the Savior taught us that we need not tolerate evil. "Jesus went into the temple of God, and . . . overthrew the tables of the moneychangers."[16] Though He loved the sinner, the Lord said that He "cannot look upon sin with the least degree of allowance."[17] His Apostle Paul specified some of those sins in a letter to the Galatians. The list included "adultery, fornication, uncleanness, lasciviousness,

"Idolatry, witchcraft, hatred, . . . wrath, strife, seditions, heresies,

"Envyings, murders, drunkenness, revellings, and such like."[18]

To Paul's list I might add the regrettable attitudes of bigotry, hypocrisy, and prejudice. These were also decried in 1834 by

71

early Church leaders who foresaw the eventual rise of this Church "amid the frowns of bigots and the calumny of hypocrites."[19] The Prophet Joseph Smith prayed that "prejudices may give way before the truth."[20] Hatred stirs up strife[21] and digs beneath the dignity of mature men and women in our enlightened era.

Paul's list included "uncleanness." As members of the Church entrusted with its holy temples, we are commanded that "no unclean thing shall be permitted to come into [His] house to pollute it."[22]

That assignment requires great fortitude as well as love. In former days, disciples of the Lord "were firm, and would suffer even unto death rather than commit sin."[23] In latter days, devoted disciples of the Lord are just as firm. Real love for the sinner may compel courageous confrontation—not acquiescence! Real love does not support self-destructing behavior.

## TOLERANCE AND MUTUAL RESPECT

Our commitment to the Savior causes us to scorn sin yet heed His commandment to love our neighbors. Together we live on this earth, which is to be tended, subdued, and shared with gratitude.[24] Each of us can help to make life in this world a more pleasant experience. In 1992, the First Presidency and the Twelve issued a public statement from which I quote: "It is morally wrong for any person or group to deny anyone his or her inalienable dignity on the tragic and abhorrent theory of racial or cultural superiority.

"We call upon all people everywhere to recommit themselves to the time-honored ideals of tolerance and mutual respect. We sincerely believe that as we acknowledge one another with consideration and compassion we will discover that we can all peacefully coexist despite our deepest differences."[25]

That pronouncement is a contemporary confirmation of the Prophet Joseph's earlier entreaty for tolerance. Unitedly we may respond. Together we may stand, intolerant of transgression but tolerant of neighbors with differences they hold sacred. Our beloved brothers and sisters throughout the world are *all* children of God. He is our Father. His Son, Jesus, is the Christ. His church has been restored to the earth in these latter days to bless all of God's children.

NOTES

1. *History of the Church,* 5:157.

2. Matthew 22:36–40; see also John 13:34–35; 15:12, 17; Romans 13:8; 1 Thessalonians 3:12; 4:9; 1 Peter 1:22; 1 John 3:11, 23; 4:7, 11–12; 2 John 1:5.

3. Mosiah 2:17.

4. Acts 10:34–35; see also D&C 38:16, 24–26.

5. Mosiah 4:14–15; see also Romans 12:18.

6. *Hymns of The Church of Jesus Christ of Latter-day Saints* (Salt Lake City: The Church of Jesus Christ of Latter-day Saints, 1985), no. 172.

7. D&C 78:14.

8. See Articles of Faith 1:13.

9. Nehemiah 6:3.

10. D&C 38:40–41; see also 88:81.

11. See Articles of Faith 1:12.

12. In Tahiti Area Conference Report, March 1976, 31.

13. 1 Peter 3:15; see also D&C 60:2.

14. Galatians 3:27–28.

15. Mosiah 18:21; see also 23:15; 4 Nephi 1:13.

16. Matthew 21:12; see also Mark 11:15.

17. D&C 1:31.

18. Galatians 5:19–21.

19. Joseph Smith—History 1:71, footnote.

20. D&C 109:56; see also verse 70.

21. See Proverbs 10:12.

22. D&C 109:20.

23. Alma 24:19.

24. See Genesis 1:28; Moses 2:28; Abraham 4:28; D&C 59:15–21.

25. Statement of the First Presidency and the Quorum of the Twelve, 18 October 1992; as quoted in *Church News*, 24 October 1992, 4.

# PART 2

CHALLENGES AND
CHOICES

# CHOICES

Not long ago a beautiful young mother asked me for guidance with a very difficult decision she was facing. It pertained to an important surgical operation that was being considered. Consequences of her choice would affect her husband and her family as well. She said, "Decisions are really hard for me. I even have trouble choosing what to wear each morning."

"You are not so different," I replied. "Each of us must make choices. That is one of life's great privileges."

I told this lovely mother that my fellow physicians are regularly asked questions about the human body. Some questions relate to surgical intervention to save a life or to save a part of the body. Other questions relate to elective procedures to alter the body's structure or function. In recent years, many questions relate to the "choice" to abort the life of a newly forming human being. Ironically, such "choice" would deny that developing individual both life and choice.

I reminded her that questions regarding our bodies represent only an important fraction of life's most challenging choices. Others include "Where shall I live?" "What shall I do with my life?" "To which cause should I commit my effort and my good name?" These are but a few of the many choices that we must make each day.

I will not disclose the name of the sister, nor the specific operation she was contemplating. To do so might divert our attention to a specific topic and away from those fundamental principles that pertain to important decisions generally.

Challenging choices face all of us from time to time. I would suggest three questions you might ask yourself as you consider your options. Whether they are once-in-a-lifetime or routine daily decisions, serious reflection on these three questions will help clarify your thinking. You might wish to review these questions:

1. *"Who am I?"*
2. *"Why am I here?"*
3. *"Where am I going?"*

Truthful answers to these three questions will remind you of important anchors and unchanging principles.

As you consider these fundamental questions, it will become clear that decisions you first thought to be purely personal virtually always impact the lives of others. In answering these questions, then, you must be mindful of the broader circle of family and friends who will be affected by the consequences of your choice. This self-evaluation will be a silent examination. No one else will hear your replies. Though I will suggest some answers, the ultimate responses must be uniquely yours.

## "WHO AM I?"

Remember, you are a son or a daughter of God. Our Heavenly Father loves you. He has created you to be successful and to have joy.

"He created man, male and female, after his own image and in his own likeness."[1]

These bodies, created in God's image, are to be preserved, protected, and well cared for. I feel as did the Apostle Paul, who likened the human body to a temple:

"Know ye not that ye are the temple of God, and that the Spirit of God dwelleth in you?

"If any man defile the temple of God, him shall God destroy; for the temple of God is holy, which temple ye are."[2]

You are one of God's noble and great spirits, held in reserve to come to earth at this time.[3] In your premortal life you were appointed to help prepare the world for the great gathering of souls that will precede the Lord's second coming. You are one of a covenant people. You are an heir to the promise that all the earth will be blessed by the seed of Abraham and that God's covenant with Abraham will be fulfilled through his lineage in these latter days.[4]

As a member of the Church, you have made sacred covenants with the Lord. You have taken upon yourself the name of Christ.[5] You have promised to always remember Him and to keep His commandments. In return, He has agreed to grant His Spirit to be with you.[6]

Having briefly considered some answers to question number one, let us turn our attention to question number two.

### "WHY AM I HERE?"

This question is one I have often asked myself. Well do I remember doing so many years ago while in military service, separated from family and friends, surrounded by the horrible devastation of war. On another unforgettable occasion, I was stranded in a cold, remote area, far from transportation, food, or shelter. No doubt you have had similar anxious moments. But those experiences are the exceptions. I'd like to discuss the greater question.

Why are you here on planet earth?

One of the most important reasons is to receive a mortal body. Another is to be tested—to experience mortality—to determine what you will do with life's challenging opportunities. Those opportunities require you to make choices, and choices depend on agency. A major reason for your mortal existence, therefore, is to test how you will exercise your agency.[7]

Agency is a divine gift to you. You are free to choose what you will be and what you will do. And you are not without help. Counsel with your parents is a privilege at any age. Prayer provides communication with your Heavenly Father and invites the promptings of personal revelation. And in certain circumstances, consultation with professional advisers and with your local leaders in the Church may be highly advisable, especially when very difficult decisions must be made.

That is precisely the pattern chosen by President Spencer W. Kimball. In 1972, Elder Kimball, then a member of the Council of the Twelve, knew that his mortal life was slipping away because of heart disease. He obtained competent medical counsel and prayerfully consulted with the Lord and with his file leaders in the Church. Elder and Sister Kimball and the First Presidency carefully weighed available alternatives. Then President Harold B. Lee, speaking for the First Presidency, counseled Elder Kimball. With great conviction, President Lee said: "Spencer, you have been called! You are not to die! You must do everything you need to do to care for yourself and continue to live."[8]

President Kimball chose to have an operation performed upon his heart that was known to carry a high risk. He was blessed with a successful result. He lived thirteen more years, eventually to succeed President Lee as President of the Church.

That precious privilege of choice—man's agency—was

decreed before the world was created.[9] It is a moral agency.[10] Thus, it was opposed by Satan,[11] but affirmed by the Lord[12] and reaffirmed through prophets in ancient and in modern times.[13]

The proper exercise of moral agency requires faith. Faith in the Lord Jesus Christ is the first principle of the gospel.[14] Because of Him, you have your agency. He must be the very foundation of your faith, and the testing of that faith is a fundamental reason for your freedom to choose.

You are free to develop and exercise faith in God and in His divine Son, faith in His word, faith in His Church, faith in His servants, and faith in His commandments.

Facing difficult challenges is neither new nor unique. Centuries ago, Joshua spoke of a choice his family faced. He declared:

"Choose you this day whom ye will serve; . . . as for me and my house, we will serve the Lord."[15]

Cultivation of that faith will entitle you to the companionship of the Holy Ghost, who will help you make wise decisions.[16]

Many may profess a measure of faith in God, but without sincere repentance, faith cannot be fully operative. This concept was made known to the Nephites:

"Many of them . . . are brought to the knowledge of the truth, . . . and are led to believe the holy scriptures, . . . which leadeth them to faith on the Lord, and unto repentance, which faith and repentance bringeth a change of heart unto them."[17]

Faith, repentance, and obedience will qualify you for sublime gifts of justice and mercy, which are bestowed upon those worthy of the blessings of the Atonement.[18]

Yes, every test, every trial, every challenge and hardship you endure is an opportunity to further develop your faith.[19]

Faith can be fortified through prayer. Prayer is the powerful key to making decisions, not only concerning your physical body, but concerning all other important aspects of your life. Humbly seek the Lord in prayer with a sincere heart and real intent, and He will help you.[20]

Remember that faith and prayer alone are seldom sufficient. Personal effort is usually necessary to accomplish your heart's desire. "Faith, if it hath not works, is dead, being alone."[21]

The answers to question number two emphasize that you are here to exercise faith, to pray, and to work hard.

Now let's turn our attention to question number three.

### "WHERE AM I GOING?"

This question reminds us that eventually you (and I) are going to die, be resurrected, be judged, and be awarded a place in eternal realms.[22] With each passing sunset, you are closer to that inevitable day of judgment. Then you will be asked to account for your faith, your hopes, and your works. The Lord said:

"Every man may act in doctrine and principle . . . according to the moral agency which I have given unto him, that every man may be accountable for his own sins in the day of judgment."[23]

As all will be resurrected, your physical body will then be restored to its proper and perfect frame.[24] The day of your resurrection will be a day of judgment that will determine the kind of life you shall have hereafter.

That judgment will consider not only your actions, but also your innermost intent and heartfelt desires. Your everyday thoughts have not been lost. Scriptures speak of the "bright recollection"[25] and "perfect remembrance"[26] that your mind will provide in times of divine judgment.

The Lord knows the desires of our hearts. At the time of judgment, surely the special yearnings of single sisters and childless couples, for example, will be given compassionate consideration by Him who said:

"I, the Lord, will judge all . . . according to their works, according to the desire of their hearts."[27]

He will know of your longings as a husband or wife—as a father or mother—who tried diligently to serve your family and society properly.

As I listen to those who argue for causes contrary to the commandments of God and observe individuals who revel in the pleasures of the world with apparent disregard for eventual judgment, I think of this divine description of their folly:

"They despised my judgments, and walked not in my statutes, . . . for their heart went after their idols."[28]

Interviews, as for temple recommends, with your bishop and members of your stake presidency are precious experiences. And, in a way, they could be considered meaningful "dress rehearsals" for that grand colloquy when you will stand before the Great Judge.

After the resurrection and judgment, you will be assigned to your everlasting home on high. The revelations liken the glory of those dwelling places to the differing lights of heavenly bodies. Paul said:

"There is one glory of the sun, and another glory of the moon, and another glory of the stars."[29]

The Lord revealed more to the Prophet Joseph Smith, who wrote of the *telestial* glory, where those will ultimately abide "who received not the gospel of Christ, neither the testimony of Jesus" while in this life.[30]

The Prophet taught of the *terrestrial* glory as the abode for the "honorable . . . of the earth, who were blinded by the craftiness of men," who rejected the gospel while on the earth.[31]

And then he wrote of the *celestial* glory, which "glory is that of the sun, even the glory of God, the highest of all."[32] There the faithful will dwell together with their families, enjoying exaltation with our Heavenly Father and His Beloved Son. With them will be those who have been obedient to ordinances and covenants made in holy temples, where they were sealed to predecessors and posterity.

As you continue to face many challenging choices in life, remember, there is great protection when you know who you are, why you are here, and where you are going. Let your unique identity shape each decision you make on the path toward your eternal destiny. Accountability for your choices now will bear on all that lies ahead.

May each of us choose wisely and with faith in Him who created us.

NOTES

1. D&C 20:18; see also Genesis 1:26–27; Mosiah 7:27; Alma 18:34; 22:12; Ether 3:15; Moses 2:27.

2. 1 Corinthians 3:16–17.

3. See D&C 86:8–11.

4. See 1 Nephi 15:18; 3 Nephi 20:25.

5. See D&C 18:28; 20:29, 37.

6. See Moroni 4:3; 5:2; D&C 20:77.

7. See 2 Nephi 2:15, 25.

8. "Spencer W. Kimball: Man of Faith," *Ensign,* December 1985, 40.

9. See D&C 93:29–31.

10. See D&C 101:78.

11. See Moses 4:3.

12. See Moses 4:2.

13. See D&C 58:26–28; Moses 6:56; 7:32.

14. See Articles of Faith 1:4.

15. Joshua 24:15; see also Moses 6:33.

16. See 2 Nephi 2:27–28; D&C 14:8.

17. Helaman 15:7.

18. See Alma 34:16–17.

19. See D&C 63:11; 101:4.

20. See Alma 33:23; Moroni 7:9; 10:4; D&C 9:7–9.

21. James 2:17; see also verses 18, 20, 26; Alma 26:22.

22. See 1 Corinthians 15:22; Alma 12:24; 21:9; Helaman 14:16–17; D&C 138:19.

23. D&C 101:78; see also Mosiah 3:24.

24. See Alma 11:43; 40:23.

25. Alma 11:43.

26. Alma 5:18.

27. D&C 137:9; see also Hebrews 4:12; Alma 18:32; D&C 6:16; 33:1; 88:109.

28. Ezekiel 20:16.

29. 1 Corinthians 15:41.

30. D&C 76:82.

31. D&C 76:75.

32. D&C 76:70.

# "THOU SHALT HAVE NO OTHER GODS"

I am reminded of military days long ago when our platoon heard shouts from a sergeant: "Attention!" "Right face!" "Left face!" "About face!" We learned to respond to those orders with instant precision. In retrospect, I don't recall ever having heard his command to "face upward." Yet scriptures tell us to "look to God and live."[1]

My topic today relates to the first of the Lord's Ten Commandments: "Thou shalt have no other gods before me."[2] This commandment may be better known than obeyed. May I share a suggestion that I have found useful in testing my own allegiance to this commandment? When confronted with a challenging choice, I ask myself, "Which way do you face?"

## LIFE WITHOUT LOOKING TO GOD

Sadly, many individuals don't know where to find God, and exclude Him from their lives. When spiritual needs arise, they may look to the left, the right, or round about. But looking to other people on the same level cannot satisfy spiritual shortages.

When the immortal spirit is starved, hunger persists for something more filling. Even when material success comes, there is a hollow ache—if living well falls short of living worthily. Inner peace cannot be found in affluence accompanied by spiritual privation.

## INVITATION TO COME TO THE LORD

Members of The Church of Jesus Christ of Latter-day Saints invite all to come unto Christ and enjoy the spiritual feast that His gospel provides. The Saints savor a sweet spiritual nourishment that sustains them through life. This sustenance comes because they have made covenants to take upon themselves the name of the Lord and strive to obey His precepts. Strength comes in recognizing and in being grateful for the Lord's gifts of immortality and the opportunity for eternal life.

## LOYAL CITIZENS

These gifts are available to all. Citizens of many countries claim membership in the Church. Regardless of their flag or form of government, they find that allegiance to the Lord does not preclude their being loyal citizens of their nations. Fidelity to God enables one to develop a more profound patriotic allegiance and become a better citizen.

In addition to their national citizenship, members of the Church are also citizens of God's kingdom.[3] Their commitment to it, however, may be variable. The great majority seek "first to build up the kingdom of God, and to establish his righteousness."[4] Some allow their allegiance to God and His kingdom to slip below that of other interests in life. They have not yet determined which way they face.[5]

## REPRESENTATIVES OF THE LORD

I perceived such confusion in the mind of a newspaper reporter who asked one of our leaders when a representative of such-and-such a country would become a General Authority. While that question was being answered, I thought about our beloved General Authorities born in the countries of Asia; of Europe; of North, Central, and South America; and of the islands of the sea. Though these Brethren come from many nations and speak several tongues, not one of them was called to represent his native country. Presiding quorums of the Church are not representative assemblies. Each leader has been called to face the people as a representative of the Lord, not the other way around.

General Authorities are "called of God, by prophecy, and by the laying on of hands by those who are in authority."[6] They are called as "especial witnesses"[7] unto *all* the world, to teach and testify of the Lord Jesus Christ.[8]

## OBEYING COMMANDMENTS OF THE LORD

No matter where we live or in what position we serve, all of us need to determine which way we face. God's commandments serve as a standard against which priorities can be measured. Our respect for the first commandment fashions our feelings for all the others. Consider the commandment to keep the Sabbath day holy, for example.[9] We live in a time when many people throughout the world have transferred their allegiance on the Sabbath from places of worship to places of amusement. Again I ask, "Which way do you face?"[10]

Scriptures give us encouragement to do right: "If thou turn away . . . from doing thy pleasure on my holy day; and call the sabbath a delight, the holy of the Lord, . . . and shalt honour him, not doing thine own ways, nor finding thine own pleasure, . . .

88

"Then shalt thou delight thyself in the Lord."[11]

Self-esteem is also earned by obedience to God's commandments regarding chastity.[12] Yet in our day, those commands have
been attacked and trivialized. The morality of self-discipline with
appropriate "denial or restraint has been popularly depicted as
unhealthy and dehumanizing." The truth is, "it is dehumanizing
to define ourselves by our desires alone."[13] Each human being is a
child of God—created in His image—with natural appetites to
control.

If we break God's first commandment, we cannot escape retribution. If we allow any other person or cause to come before
allegiance to Him, we will reap a bitter harvest. Paul foresaw
"destruction" for those "whose God is their belly."[14] (I might
include all forms of anatomical affection.) Any who choose to
serve "the creature more than the Creator"[15] deprive themselves
of spiritual reward.

Thus, our priorities should be honestly evaluated in terms of
that first commandment. If change in direction is needed, we
may want to issue a self-command to "about face!" Doing so
would please the Lord, who said, "Repent, and turn yourselves
from your idols; and turn away your faces from all your abomi-
nations."[16]

Trees reach up for the light and grow in the process. So do
we as sons and daughters of heavenly parents. Facing upward
provides a loftier perspective than facing right or facing left.
Looking up in search of holiness builds strength and dignity as
disciples of Deity.[17]

## FACING OUR FAMILIES

Facing upward is crucial for successful parenting. Families
deserve guidance from heaven. Parents cannot counsel children
adequately from personal experience, fear, or sympathy.[18] But

when parents face children as would the Creator who gave them life, parents will be endowed with wisdom beyond that of their own. Wise mothers and fathers will teach members of their family how to make personal decisions based upon divine law.[19] They will teach them that "this life is the time . . . to prepare to meet God."[20] They will teach them that decisions of a moral and spiritual character *cannot* be based on freedom to choose without accountability to God for those choices.[21] With that understanding, parents and children will be rewarded with strength of character, peace of mind, joy, and rejoicing in their posterity.[22]

### FACING OUR NEIGHBORS

Similarly, relationships with neighbors, friends, and associates will be enhanced as we approach them with "the pure love of Christ."[23] A desire to emulate the Lord provides powerful motivation for good. Our craving for compassion will cause us to act in accord with the Golden Rule.[24] By so doing, we will find joy in feeding the poor, clothing the naked, or doing volunteer work of worth.

Service to neighbors takes on new stature when we first look to God. In the Church, when priesthood and auxiliary leaders face their congregations, quorums, and classes as would the Lord, they learn that it does not matter *where* they serve, but *how*. Position in the Church does not exalt anyone, but faithfulness does. On the other hand, aspiring to a visible position—striving to become a master rather than a servant—can destroy the spirit of the worker and the work.

Occasionally confusion exists regarding servants and masters. The Bible reports that a group of men "had disputed among themselves, who should be the greatest" among them. Jesus said, "If any man desire to be first, the same shall be last of all, and *servant of all*."[25]

Was Jesus asking His disciples to respond to random requests from the crowd or to serve tables?[26] No! He was asking them to serve in *His* way. The people were not to be masters of His disciples. The *Lord* is their Master.

In rendering service to others, which way do we face? From the right or the left, we can only push or pull. We can lift only from a higher plane. To reach it, we don't look sideways; we look up to our Master. Just as we must look to God to *live* well, so we must look to God to *serve* well.

## ATTITUDES OF EFFECTIVE DISCIPLES

If we are called to positions of leadership, we are accountable to the Savior for the acts we perform in that office. Those actions are shaped by attitudes, and attitudes are elevated while lowering our heads in humble prayer. So state words in the hymn "Before Thee, Lord, I Bow My Head":

> Look up, my soul; be not cast down.
> Keep not thine eyes upon the ground.
> Break off the shackles of the earth.
> Receive, my soul, the spirit's birth.
> And now as I go forth again
> To mingle with my fellowmen,
> Stay thou nearby, my steps to guide,
> That I may in thy love abide.[27]

Praying helps us to face trials in life. Prayer centers our attitudes precisely. With that focus, we do not wander to the right or left through land mined with traps of temptation. Disciples do not flirt with danger at the jagged edge of disaster. Experienced mountain climbers do not lean toward the dangerous edge but toward safety, with ropes and other safeguards to secure them to those they trust. So it is with us. When we climb mountainous challenges of life, we should lean toward our Master and be yoked with Him, clinging tightly to the iron rod of the gospel, to family, and to trusted friends.

President David O. McKay taught this about edges: "Many of us through selfishness are lingering near the edge of the animal jungle where Nature's law demands us to do everything with self in view."[28]

The Lord said, "Look unto me in every thought; doubt not, fear not."[29] I have learned that such faith gives emancipating power. Facing God first lets us decide firmly what we shall not do; then we are free to pursue what we ought to do.

President Gordon B. Hinckley has declared: "Love of God is the root of all virtue, of all goodness, of all strength of character, of all fidelity to do right. Love the Lord your God, and love his Son, and be ever grateful for their love for us. Whenever other love fades, there will be that shining, transcendent, everlasting love of God for each of us and the love of his Son, who gave his life for us."[30]

Race, nationality, occupation, or other interests need not stand in the way. All can look to the Lord. All can place Him first in their lives. Those who do so and remain faithful will qualify for His sublime promise:[31] "Every soul who forsaketh his sins and cometh unto me, and calleth on my name, and obeyeth my voice, and keepeth my commandments, shall see my face and know that I am."[32] This glorious destiny can be ours.

NOTES

1. Alma 37:47; see also Psalm 5:3; Alma 5:19; 37:37.

2. Exodus 20:3; see also D&C 20:17–19.

3. See Ephesians 2:19.

4. JST, Matthew 6:38.

5. See Joel 3:14.

6. Articles of Faith 1:5.

7. D&C 107:25.

8. What they speak "when moved upon by the Holy Ghost" represents the will of the Lord, the mind of the Lord, and the word of the Lord (D&C 68:4).

9. Among the many, see Exodus 20:8; 31:15; 35:2; Leviticus 23:3; Jarom 1:5; Mosiah 13:16; 18:23; D&C 68:29.

10. See 1 Kings 18:21.

11. Isaiah 58:13–14.

12. Some of the many are Exodus 20:14; Leviticus 18:22; Matthew 5:28; 1 Corinthians 6:9; 3 Nephi 12:28; D&C 42:24; 59:6.

13. Report of the Ramsey Colloquium, *Wall Street Journal,* 24 February 1994, A–18.

14. Philippians 3:19.

15. Romans 1:25.

16. Ezekiel 14:6.

17. The importance of looking up to the Lord is also emphasized in a vision to the Prophet Joseph Smith, dated 21 January 1836:

"I saw the Twelve Apostles of the Lamb, who are now upon the earth, who hold the keys of this last ministry, in foreign lands, standing together in a circle, much fatigued, with their clothes tattered and feet swollen, with their eyes cast downward, and Jesus standing in their midst, and they did not behold Him. The Savior looked upon them and wept" (*Teachings of the Prophet Joseph Smith,* 107).

That the Twelve were subsequently vindicated is apparent as we read further in the Prophet's record: "And I finally saw the Twelve in the celestial kingdom of God. I also beheld the redemption of Zion, and many things which the tongue of men cannot describe in full" (*Teachings of the Prophet Joseph Smith,* 108).

18. See Proverbs 3:5.

19. See D&C 130:20–21, which teaches that any blessing from God is obtained by obedience to that law upon which the blessing is predicated.

20. See Alma 34:32.

21. See D&C 101:78.

22. JST, Genesis 9:22 adds this insight: "When thy posterity shall embrace

the truth, and look upward, then shall Zion look downward, and all the heavens shall shake with gladness, and the earth shall tremble with joy."

23. Moroni 7:47.

24. "Whatsoever ye would that men should do to you, do ye even so to them" (Matthew 7:12).

25. Mark 9:34–35; emphasis added. Another gospel writer phrased that truth in a similar way: "He that is greatest among you shall be your servant" (Matthew 23:11). In these scriptures, the word *servant* comes from the Greek noun *diakonos,* which means "one who executes the commands of another, especially of a master." *Diakonos* is the Greek word from which the English word *deacon* is derived.

26. See Acts 6:2.

27. *Hymns,* no. 158.

28. *Improvement Era,* June 1957, 390. President James E. Faust issued this solemn warning: "Living on the edge can also mean being perilously close to the Bottomless Pit. . . .

"Some of you may think that you will discover your strengths and abilities by living on the edge. . . . There will always be enough risks that will come to you naturally without your having to seek them out" (*Ensign,* November 1995, 46).

29. D&C 6:36.

30. Ricks College regional conference, 29 Oct. 1995; reported in *Church News,* 2 Mar. 1996, 2.

31. He has also given many others, among which are:

• "Blessed are you; for as you now behold me and know that I am, even so shall ye come unto me and your souls shall live" (D&C 45:46).

• "I will go before your face. I will be on your right hand and on your left, and my Spirit shall be in your hearts, and mine angels round about you, to bear you up" (D&C 84:88).

32. D&C 93:1.

# ADDICTION OR FREEDOM

I am impressed to address a problem of deep concern—the worldwide epidemic of drug addiction. As a medical doctor, I began my study of drugs early in medical school. Each doctor spends months in specialized courses learning potential benefits and risks of medicinal agents. Proper prescription of drugs is the forte of skilled physicians. Generally, when their advice is carefully followed, results are remarkably successful. In addressing this topic, I specifically exclude such application of modern knowledge by educated professionals.

But I raise my voice with others throughout the world who warn against abuse of drugs beyond prescribed limits, and the recreational or social use of chemical substances so often begun naively by the ill-informed.

From an initial experiment thought to be trivial, a vicious cycle may follow. From trial comes a habit. From habit comes dependence. From dependence comes addiction. Its grasp is so gradual. Enslaving shackles of habit are too small to be sensed until they are too strong to be broken. Indeed, drugs are the modern "mess of pottage" for which souls are sold. No families are free from risk.

But this problem is broader than hard drugs. Their use most

often begins with cigarette smoking.[1] Tobacco and alcoholic beverages contain addicting drugs. They lead the list in incidence and cost to society.

As I speak with governmental and medical leaders of many nations, they voice grave concern over the consumption of alcohol and other substances by their citizens. Though the extent of the challenge is international, I will cite data from the United States of America solely to indicate the monstrous scope of this worldwide problem.

## TOBACCO

Consider the magnitude of tobacco's harm. Cigarette smoking is the most frequent preventable cause of heart disease, artery disease, lung disease, and cancer.[2] In the United States in 1982, 16 percent of all deaths (314,000) were attributed to the smoking of tobacco.[3]

For the year 1985, the estimated cost of both smoking-related health care and lost productivity amounted to $65 billion. That calculates to an average of $2.17 per pack of cigarettes sold.[4] Social consequences of smoking far exceed the price paid to purchase cigarettes.

An insurance company recently reported that one-fifth of all its claims were for afflictions that could have been prevented by simply not smoking.[5] We all bear this financial burden of illness that need not be.

In 1988, Dr. C. Everett Koop—then surgeon general of the United States—and his team of more than fifty scientists published a landmark report. For the United States alone, they attributed 320,000 deaths annually to tobacco, 125,000 to alcohol, and lesser mortality to cocaine (2,000) and other opioids (4,000). They declared nicotine to be a powerfully addicting drug in the same sense as are drugs such as heroin and cocaine.[6]

Comparable views have been recorded by medical authorities in many other nations.[7] Yet many of our good friends who use tobacco may not believe it to be addicting. Some are reluctant to admit that their behavior is substantially controlled by a drug. We understand those feelings.

## ALCOHOL

There is mounting concern worldwide over the consumption of alcohol. The U.S. government estimates that 10.6 million adults are alcoholics and that one family in four is troubled by alcohol.[8] It is a factor in half of all the nation's traffic deaths.[9]

In 1987, a tragic milestone was reached. More Americans had been killed from alcohol-related motor vehicle accidents (1,350,000) than had been killed in all the wars America has ever fought (1,156,000).[10]

## OTHER DRUGS

Drugs such as LSD, marijuana, heroin, and cocaine are also endangering people throughout the earth. The noble attributes of reason, integrity, and dignity, which distinguish men and women from all other forms of life, are often the first to be attacked by these drugs and alcohol.

## REACHING HELP

We reach out in love to family, friends, and neighbors, regardless of nationality or creed, who suffer addiction. The Church of Jesus Christ of Latter-day Saints continues to help relieve this international plague.

The solution to this problem ultimately is neither governmental nor institutional. Nor is it a question of legality. It is a matter of individual choice and commitment. Agency must be understood. The importance of the will in making crucial choices must be known. Then steps toward relief can follow.

## AGENCY

Agency, or the power to choose, was ours as spirit children of our Creator before the world was.[11] It is a gift from God, nearly as precious as life itself.

Often, however, agency is misunderstood. While we are free to choose, once we have made those choices, we are tied to the consequences of those choices.

We are free to take drugs or not. But once we choose to use a habit-forming drug, we are bound to the consequences of that choice. Addiction surrenders later freedom to choose. Through chemical means, one can literally become disconnected from his or her own will!

## ROAD TO RECOVERY

For relief of an ailment, as a doctor of medicine I might write a prescription. As an ordained Apostle, I would invoke the spiritual blessing of eternal perspective. Combined, my spiritual prescription would return the gift of agency to its rightful owner.

Each one who resolves to climb that steep road to recovery must gird up for the fight of a lifetime. But a lifetime is a prize well worth the price.

This challenge uniquely involves the will, and the will can prevail. Healing doesn't come after the first dose of any medicine. So the prescription must be followed firmly, bearing in mind that it often takes as long to recover as it did to become ill. But if made consistently and persistently, correct choices can cure.

## SPIRITUAL PRESCRIPTION

My spiritual prescription includes six choices which I shall list alphabetically, **A** through **F,** and then comment about each:

Choose to be **A**live

Choose to **B**elieve

Choose to **C**hange

Choose to be **D**ifferent

Choose to **E**xercise

Choose to be **F**ree

**1. Choose to be Alive.** Seek beloved family, friends, and physicians. Plead for their help. Your precious life is at stake. "Cheer up your hearts, and remember that ye are free to act for yourselves—to choose the way of everlasting death or the way of eternal life."[12]

The choice for life brings an outlook of optimism. It breathes hope. It rekindles self-esteem—regarding one's body as a timeless trust. And it awakens a personal commitment to "see that ye take care of these sacred things, . . . that ye look to God and live."[13]

**2. Choose to Believe.** Believe in God. Accept yourself as His child, created in His image. He loves you and wants you to be happy. He wants you to grow through life's choices and become more like Him. He pleads that you will "reconcile [yourself] to the will of God, and not to the will of the . . . flesh."[14]

Reconciliation requires faith, repentance, and baptism. Be "born of God, changed from [your] carnal and fallen state, to a state of righteousness."[15] Renew covenants made at baptism by worthily partaking of the sacrament regularly, "that thou mayest more fully keep thyself unspotted from the world."[16]

Then "be meek and lowly in heart. . . . Withstand every temptation of the devil, with . . . faith on the Lord Jesus Christ."[17]

Choose to believe in and be blessed by your Creator.

**3. Choose to Change.** "How long will ye suffer [yourself] to be led by foolish and blind guides? Yea, how long will ye choose darkness rather than light?"[18] Choose to change—today!

"The spirit and the body are the soul of man."[19] Both spirit and body have appetites. One of life's great challenges is to develop dominance of spiritual appetites over those that are physical. Your willpower becomes strong when joined with the will of the Lord.

Addiction to any substance enslaves not only the physical body but the spirit as well. Therefore, repentance is best achieved while one still has a body to help attain spiritual supremacy:

"This life is the time for men to prepare to meet God; . . . this life is the day for men to perform their labors. . . .

"Do not procrastinate the day of your repentance; . . . if we do not improve our time while in this life, then cometh the night of darkness wherein there can be no labor performed. . . .

"That same spirit which doth possess your bodies at the time that ye go out of this life . . . will have power to possess your body in that eternal world."[20]

To be carnally minded is death, but to be spiritually minded is life eternal.[21] That blessing will come to those with the will to change.

**4. Choose to be Different.** Distinguish yourself from worldly crowds. Defenders do not resemble offenders. Among them are clever merchandisers who plot to link beer with sports, tobacco with charm, and drugs with fun. Scripture warns of those who so deceive:

"Thus saith the Lord unto you: In consequence of evils and designs which do and will exist in the hearts of conspiring men in the last days, I have warned you, and forewarn you, by giving unto you this word of wisdom by revelation."[22]

His Word of Wisdom includes sound nutritional guidance and simple instructions. We are not to drink alcoholic beverages.[23] We are not to use tobacco.[24] We are not to drink tea or coffee.[25] And in this same spirit, we are not to use addicting drugs.[26]

So to modern Israel, God has given modern counsel, similar to ancient commandments recorded in the Old Testament:

"It is not for kings to drink wine; nor for princes strong drink:

"Lest they drink, and forget the law."[27]

"Woe unto him that giveth his neighbour drink, that puttest thy bottle to him, and makest him drunken."[28]

Certainly modern medical research validates the physical benefits of obedience to the Word of Wisdom. The evidence is so great that many will be taught the right things for only half of the right reasons. With that limited understanding, could they then try a smoke, a drink, or a drug, rationalizing that "just one won't hurt"? Could the prospect of only future physical rewards even be bait for foolish dares of defiance now? Or to phrase these questions another way, how many would be *determined* to obey the will of the Lord even if physical benefits were *not* assured? When God asked Abraham to offer Isaac in sacrifice, did they first seek scientific confirmation that their choice to obey was medically advisable?

The Word of Wisdom is a spiritual law. To the obedient He proclaimed: "I, the Lord, give unto them a promise, that the destroying angel shall pass by them, as the children of Israel, and not slay them."[29]

At the first passover, the destroying angel did pass over houses that were marked with blood on the doorposts. In our day, the faithful keep the Word of Wisdom. It is one of our signs unto God that we are His covenant people.

101

Choose to be different; you will be blessed both physically and spiritually.

**5. Choose to Exercise.** Exercising the body and the spirit will aid in the climb toward recovery. Appropriate physical activity helps to combat depression, which so often accompanies addiction.

But spiritual exercise is even more crucial. This battle will be more easily won with fervent prayer. If we truly "counsel with the Lord in all [our] doings, . . . he will direct [us] for good."[30]

Strength comes from uplifting music, good books, and feasting from the scriptures. Since the Book of Mormon was to come forth "when there shall be great pollutions upon the face of the earth,"[31] study of that book in particular will fortify us.

Exercise the body and the spirit and choose to exercise faith in God.

**6. Choose to be Free.** Break "bands of iniquity."[32] Leave behind "an iron yoke, . . . handcuffs, and chains, and shackles, and fetters of hell."[33]

Choose to be free from feigned friends who first flatter yet later despise.[34] Drug abuse may have started with them, but you pay the price.

"Remember, my brethren [and sisters], that whosoever perisheth, perisheth unto himself; and whosoever doeth iniquity, doeth it unto himself; for behold, ye are free; ye are permitted to act for yourselves; for behold, God hath given unto you a knowledge and he hath made you free."[35]

The Lord has revealed His sacred standard to guide people in a troubled world. You and I were born free to follow His divine guidance. We may choose for ourselves. Those choices may bring addiction or freedom. For freedom and joy, choose to "be faithful in Christ." He will lift you up. May "the hope of his glory and of eternal life, rest in your mind forever."[36]

102

NOTES

1. *The Health Consequences of Smoking: Nicotine Addiction,* Public Health Service, U.S. Government Printing Office, 1988, 262–63.

2. *Cigarette Smoking and Cardiovascular Disease 1985: Special Report to the Public,* American Heart Association (50–075-A).

3. Office of Technology Assessment, U.S. Congress Staff Memorandum, September 1985, 2.

4. Ibid., 5.

5. *Utah Hospital Leaders Digest,* 15 July 1988, 2.

6. *The Health Consequences of Smoking: Nicotine Addiction,* Public Health Service, U.S. Government Printing Office, 1988, 14, 334.

7. Among them are Nigel Gray, director, Anti-Cancer Council, Victoria, Australia; David Simpson, director, Action on Smoking and Health, U.K.; Pamela Taylor, spokesperson, British Medical Association, U.K.; Andrew Pipe, University of Ottawa Heart Institute, Canada; Roberta Ferrence, Addiction Research Foundation, Canada; Bernie McKay, secretary, Commonwealth Department of Health, Australia. *Times and Seasons,* Documentary on Tobacco, July 1988.

8. "Coming to Grips with Alcoholism," *U.S. News and World Report,* 30 November 1987, 56–57.

9. *Healthy People: The Surgeon General's Report on Health Promotion and Disease Prevention,* Public Health Service, U.S. Government Printing Office, 1979, 125.

10. *Accident Facts,* Annual Report of the National Safety Council, 1975, confirmed by telephone conversation 20 July 1988.

11. See Alma 13:3; Moses 4:4.

12. 2 Nephi 10:23.

13. Alma 37:47.

14. 2 Nephi 10:24.

15. Mosiah 27:25.

16. D&C 59:9.

17. Alma 37:33.

18. Helaman 13:29.

19. D&C 88:15.

20. Alma 34:32–34.

21. See 2 Nephi 9:39; Romans 8:6.

22. D&C 89:4.

23. See D&C 89:5–7.

24. See D&C 89:8.

25. D&C 89:9.

26. Ezra Taft Benson, *Ensign,* May 1983, 54–55; Spencer W. Kimball, *Ensign,* May 1974, 7; Joseph Fielding Smith, *Ensign,* June 1971, 49; Heber J. Grant, J. Reuben Clark, Jr., David O. McKay, "Message of the First Presidency," in Conference Report, October 1942, 4–17.

27. Proverbs 31:4–5.

28. Habakkuk 2:15; see also Proverbs 20:1.

29. D&C 89:21.

30. Alma 37:37.

31. Mormon 8:31.

32. Mosiah 23:12; see also 1 Nephi 13:5.

33. D&C 123:8.

34. D&C 121:20.

35. Helaman 14:30.

36. Moroni 9:25.

# "WITH GOD NOTHING SHALL BE IMPOSSIBLE"

I applaud the efforts of Latter-day Saints throughout the world who willingly serve in building the kingdom of God. Like-wise, I respect those who quietly do their duty though deepening trials come their way. And I admire those who strive to be more worthy by overcoming a personal fault or who work to achieve a difficult goal.

I feel impressed to counsel those engaged in personal challenges to do right. In particular, my heart reaches out to those who feel discouraged by the magnitude of their struggle. Many shoulder heavy burdens of righteous responsibility which, on occasion, seem so difficult to bear. I have heard those challenges termed *impossible*.

As a medical doctor, I have known the face of adversity. I have seen much of death and dying, suffering and sorrow. I also remember the plight of students overwhelmed by their studies and of those striving to learn a foreign language. And I recall the fatigue and frustration felt by young parents with children in need. Amidst circumstances seemingly impossible, I have also experienced the joyous relief that comes when one's under-standing is deepened by scriptural insight.

The Lord has often chosen to instruct His people in their times of trial. Scriptures show that some of His lasting lessons have been taught with examples terrible as war, commonplace as childbearing, or obvious as hazards of deep water. His teachings are frequently based on common understanding, but with un-common results. Indeed, one might say that to teach His people, the Lord employs the unlikely.

Warfare, for example, has been known since time began. Even in that ugly circumstance, the Lord has helped those obe-dient to His counsel. Going into battle, all would assume the obvious advantage of outnumbering an enemy. But when God's disciple Gideon was leading an army against the Midianites, "the Lord said unto Gideon, The people that are with thee are too many . . . , lest Israel vaunt themselves . . . , saying, Mine own hand hath saved me."[1]

So the Lord directed Gideon to reduce his numbers. He first decreased the troops from twenty-two thousand to ten thousand.

Then the Lord said to Gideon, "The people are yet too many."[2] So another reduction was made. Finally, only three hun-dred remained. Then the Lord delivered the victory to the out-numbered few.[3]

Even more widely known than war is an understanding of childbearing. Everyone "knows" that *old* women do not bear chil-dren. So upon whom did the Lord call to bear Abraham's birthright son? Sarah, at age ninety! When told this was to be, she asked a logical question: "Shall I [which am old] of a surety bear a child?"[4] From heaven came this reply: "Is any thing too hard for the Lord?"[5]

So decreed, she gave birth to Isaac, to carry the crucial Abra-hamic covenant into the second generation.[6]

Later, for one of the most important events ever to occur, the other extreme was chosen. As all knew that an elderly woman could not bear children, it was just as obvious that a virgin could not have children. But Isaiah had made this prophetic utterance:

"The Lord himself shall give you a sign; Behold, a virgin shall conceive, and bear a son, and shall call his name Immanuel."[7]

When Mary was notified of her sacred responsibility, the announcing angel reassured, "For with God nothing shall be impossible."[8]

The expression *deep water* means danger! That very hazard challenged the Israelites led by Moses at the Red Sea.[9] Later, they were led by Joshua to the river Jordan at flood time.[10] In each instance, deep water was divinely divided to allow the faithful to reach their destination safely. To teach His people, the Lord employs the unlikely.

Turning to our day, have you ever wondered why the Master waited so long to inaugurate the promised "restitution of all things"?[11] Any competitor knows the disadvantage of allowing an opponent to get too far ahead. Wouldn't the work of the restoration of the Church have been easier if begun earlier?

Suppose for a moment you are a member of a team. The coach beckons you from the bench and says: "You are to enter this contest. I not only want you to win; you shall win. But the going will be tough. The score at this moment is 1,143,000,000 to 6, and you are to play on the team with the 6 points!"

That large number was the approximate population of the earth in the year 1830 when the restored Church of Jesus Christ was officially organized with six members.[12] The setting was remote and rural. By standards of the world, its leaders were deemed to be unlearned. Their followers seemed so ordinary.

But with them, the work was begun. Assignments had been revealed:

• The gospel was to be preached to every kindred, nation, tongue, and people.

• Ordinary folk were to become Saints.

• Redemptive work was to be done for all who had ever lived.

The great dispensation of the latter days had commenced, and they were the ones to usher it forth!

Furthermore, the Prophet Joseph Smith was unjustly held in the unspeakable isolation of a distant prison. In such obscurity, then and there, he was told by the Lord that "the ends of the earth shall inquire after thy name."[13]

If any tasks ever deserved the label *impossible,* those would seem to qualify. But, in fact, our Lord had spoken: "With men this is impossible; but with God all things are possible."[14] To teach His people, the Lord employs the unlikely.

A century and a half later, the burdening baton of that opportunity has now been passed to us. We are children of the noble birthright, who must carry on in spite of our foredetermined status to be broadly outnumbered and widely opposed. Challenges lie ahead for the Church and for each member divinely charged toward self-improvement and service.

How is it possible to achieve the "impossible"? Learn and obey the teachings of God. From the holy scriptures, heaven-sent lift will be found for heaven-sent duties. To so achieve, at least three basic scriptural themes loom repeatedly as requirements.

## FAITH

The foremost requisite is *faith.* It is the first principle of the gospel.[15] In his epistle to the Hebrews, Paul so taught. He concluded that by faith the great deeds of Noah, Abraham, Sarah,

108

Isaac, Jacob, Joseph, Moses, Joshua, and others were accomplished.[16]

Prophets on the American hemisphere similarly taught the fundamental importance of faith. Moroni said it included things "hoped for and not seen" and then warned his skeptics, "Dispute not because ye see not, for ye receive no witness until after the trial of your faith."[17] Then he spoke of leaders whose faith preceded their miraculous deeds, including Alma, Amulek, Nephi, Lehi, Ammon, the brother of Jared, and the three who were promised that they should not taste of death.[18]

The Lord personally taught this truth to His disciples: "If ye have faith," He said, "nothing shall be impossible unto you."[19]

Faith is nurtured through knowledge of God. It comes from prayer and feasting upon the words of Christ through diligent study of the scriptures.

## Focus

The second requisite I have classified as *focus*. Imagine, if you will, a pair of powerful binoculars. Two separate optical systems are joined together with a gear to focus two independent images into one three-dimensional view. To apply this analogy, let the scene on the left side of your binoculars represent *your perception* of your task. Let the picture on the right side represent the *Lord's perspective* of your task—the portion of His plan He has entrusted to you. Now, connect your system to His. By mental adjustment, fuse your focus. Something wonderful happens. Your vision and His are now the same. You have developed an "eye single to the glory of God."[20] With that perspective, look upward—above and beyond mundane things about you.

The Lord said, "Look unto me in every thought."[21] That special vision will also help clarify your wishes when they may be a bit fuzzy and out of focus with God's hopes for your divine destiny. Indeed, the precise challenge you regard now as "impossible" may be the very refinement you need, in His eye.

Recently I visited the home of a man terminally ill. The stake president introduced me to the man's family. His wife demonstrated such focus when she asked for a blessing for her dying husband—not for healing, but for peace, not for a miracle, but for ability to abide to the end. She could see from an eternal viewpoint, not merely from the perspective of one weighted with the responsibilities of her husband's day-to-day care.

Elsewhere, a mother with focus nurtures her son, crippled for the whole of this life. Daily, she thanks her Heavenly Father for the privilege of laboring in love with a child for whom mortality's vale of tears will be mercifully brief. Her focus is fixed on eternity. When we have celestial sight, trials impossible to change become possible to endure.

### STRENGTH AND COURAGE

A third theme in the scriptures requisite for significant accomplishment is difficult to summarize in one word, so I shall link two to describe it—*strength* and *courage*. Repeatedly, scriptures yoke these attributes of character together, especially when difficult challenges are to be conquered.[22]

Perhaps this is more easily illustrated than defined. Our pioneer forefathers are good examples. They sang, "Gird up your loins; fresh courage take."[23] They feared no toil and no labor. Among them were Johan Andreas Jensen and his wife, Petra, who left their native Norway in 1863. Their family included six-week-old tiny twin daughters. As handcarts were pulled in their rugged journey, one of those little girls died along the way. The child who survived grew up to become my Grandmother Nelson!

There are pioneers in the Church today just as strong and

courageous. Recently, I interviewed a married couple three days after their release as full-time missionaries in a large metropolis. "We are converts," they said. "We joined the Church ten years ago. Even though we just completed a mission, we want to go again! But this time, we would like to volunteer for a more difficult assignment. We want to teach and serve children of God who live in remote areas of the world!"

As I countered with the grim realities of their request, they continued their expression of commitment. "Our three children and their spouses will assist with our expenses. Two of those couples have joined the Church already, and the third is equally supportive. Please send us among humble people who love the Lord and desire to know that His church has again been restored to the earth." Needless to say, their petition was gratefully heard, and now they have received their second call to missionary service.

Strength and courage also characterize another couple. As faithful members of the Church, they had always upheld its doctrines, including the twelfth article of faith. When their country went to war, military conscription called the dutiful husband away from his wife before either had learned she was to bear their child. He was captured by enemy troops and taken as a prisoner of war. Months elapsed. Their baby came. Still no word to know whether the new father was alive. A year after his capture, he was permitted to write to his wife.

Meanwhile, though countries apart, they each remained faithful to covenants made at baptism. Even though clothed in prisoner's stripes and able to speak the language of his captors' country only in a limited way, he became Sunday School superintendent of the branch. He baptized four fellow prisoners during their confinement. Three years after the war ended, he returned home to his wife and a son he had never seen. Later, he served for ten years as the first stake president of his country. Later he served as a member of the presidency of one of our temples! His wife stood faithfully beside him in the privilege of those sacred assignments.

You who may be momentarily disheartened, remember, life is not meant to be easy. Trials must be borne and grief endured along the way. As you remember that "with God nothing shall be impossible,"[24] know that He is your Father. You are a son or daughter created in His image, entitled through your worthiness to receive revelation to help with your righteous endeavors. You may take upon you the holy name of the Lord. You can qualify to speak in the sacred name of God.[25] It matters not that giants of tribulation torment you. Your prayerful access to help is just as real as when David battled his Goliath.[26]

Foster your faith. Fuse your focus with an eye single to the glory of God. "Be strong and courageous,"[27] and you will be given power and protection from on high. "For I will go before your face," the Lord declared. "I will be on your right hand and on your left, and my Spirit shall be in your hearts, and mine angels round about you, to bear you up."[28]

The great latter-day work of which we are a part shall be accomplished. Prophecies of the ages shall be fulfilled. "For with God all things are possible."[29]

NOTES

1. Judges 7:2.
2. Judges 7:4.
3. See Judges 7:5–25.
4. Genesis 18:13.
5. Genesis 18:14.
6. See Genesis 26:1–4, 24.
7. Isaiah 7:14.

8. Luke 1:37.

9. See Exodus 14.

10. See Joshua 3.

11. Acts 3:21.

12. See James Avery Joyce, sel., *World Population Basic Documents,* 4 vols. (Dobbs Ferry, New York: Oceana Publications, 1976), 4:2214.

13. D&C 122:1.

14. Matthew 19:26; see also Mark 10:27; Luke 18:27.

15. See Articles of Faith 1:4.

16. See Hebrews 11:4–34.

17. Ether 12:6.

18. See Ether 12:13–20.

19. Matthew 17:20.

20. D&C 4:5; see also Mormon 8:15.

21. D&C 6:36.

22. See Deuteronomy 31:6, 7, 23; Joshua 1:6, 7, 9, 18; 10:25; 1 Chronicles 22:13; 28:20; 2 Chronicles 32:7; Psalm 27:14; 31:24; Alma 43:43; 53:20.

23. "Come, Come, Ye Saints," *Hymns,* no. 30.

24. Luke 1:37.

25. See D&C 1:20.

26. See 1 Samuel 17.

27. 2 Chronicles 32:7.

28. D&C 84:88.

29. Mark 10:27.

# "A More Excellent Hope"

M oroni, a Book of Mormon prophet, declared that "man might have a more excellent hope; wherefore man must *hope,* or he cannot receive an inheritance in the place which [God has] prepared."[1]

That verse of scripture came to mind one day as I read a letter from a troubled friend who was wrestling with a profound personal problem. I would like to quote excerpts from that letter:[2]

"The guilt and failure I feel make it almost impossible for me to repent. I am losing my faith. The sins were first; the doubts followed. The order is important because sin needed doubt. When I doubted my faith, sins lost their meaning and guilt its bite. Doubting began, then, as a means of anesthesia. It served to diminish the guilt that was literally tearing me apart. Before long, however, the doubts thrived independent of the needs that conceived them.

"My painful indecisiveness, my tentativeness, my lack of direction, my paralysis of volition, my poverty of confidence, have caused suffering and depression. My family, my future, and my faith are at stake. I am losing hope."

Could the author of that letter, as well as others with such inner turmoil, have forgotten a promise of the Lord? He said, "Let virtue garnish thy thoughts unceasingly; then shall thy confidence wax strong in the presence of God."[3] Unrighteous thoughts are the termites of character—and of confidence.

To the author of the letter and to each person reading my words, I bring a message of hope. Regardless of how desperate things may seem, remember—we can always have hope. Always! The Lord's promise to us is certain: "He that endureth in faith and doeth my will, the same shall overcome."[4] I repeat—there is always hope!

We came to the earth to receive our bodies and to be tested. Do we remember the scripture that states, "We will prove them herewith, to see if they will do all things whatsoever the Lord their God shall command them"?[5] Passing tests of obedience requires faith and hope—constantly.

Hope is part of our religion and is mentioned in one of the Articles of Faith. "We follow the admonition of Paul—We believe all things, we *hope* all things, we have endured many things, and *hope* to be able to endure all things."[6]

A correlation exists between hope and gratitude. To illustrate, let me share a personal experience. For Thanksgiving a few years ago, Sister Nelson and I hosted a memorable family gathering. All of our locally available daughters, sons, and grandchildren were there, among others. We counted sixty-three people at the feast. As part of our after-dinner program, Sister Nelson distributed to each individual a sheet of paper headed, "This year, I am thankful for . . ." The remainder of the page was blank. She asked each to complete the thought, either in writing or by drawing a picture. The papers were then collected, redistributed, and read aloud. We were asked to guess who composed each reply, which, incidentally, was not very difficult.

Meanwhile, I observed a pattern. Generally, the children

were thankful for food, clothing, shelter, and family. Their pictures were precious, though not likely to be shown in an art gallery. Our youth broadened their expressions to include gratitude for their country, freedom, and church. The adults noted most of those items, but in addition mentioned the temple, their love of the Lord, and appreciation for His atonement. Their hopes were combined with gratitude. Counting blessings is better than recounting problems.

Hope emanates from the Lord, and it transcends the bounds of this mortal sphere. Paul noted that "if in this life only we have hope in Christ, we are of all men most miserable."[7] Only with an eternal perspective of God's great plan of happiness can we ever find a more excellent hope. "What is it that ye shall hope for?" asked Mormon. He then answered his own question: "Behold I say unto you that ye shall have hope through the atonement of Christ."[8] Have you heard the old statement that "hope springs eternal"?[9] It can be true only if that hope springs from Him who is eternal.

### FAITH, HOPE, AND CHARITY

Have you noticed in the scriptures that hope seldom stands alone? Hope is often linked with faith. Hope and faith are commonly connected to charity. Why? Because hope is essential to faith; faith is essential to hope; faith and hope are essential to charity.[10] They support one another like legs on a three-legged stool. All three relate to our Redeemer.

*Faith* is rooted in Jesus Christ. *Hope* centers in His atonement. *Charity* is manifest in the "pure love of Christ."[11] These three attributes are intertwined like strands in a cable and may not always be precisely distinguished. Together, they become our tether to the celestial kingdom.

We read in the Book of Mormon: "There must be faith; and

if there must be faith there must also be hope; and if there must be hope there must also be charity.

"And except ye have charity ye can in nowise be saved in the kingdom of God; neither can ye be saved in the kingdom of God if ye have not faith; neither can ye if ye have no hope."[12]

We know that there is an opposition in all things.[13] Not surprisingly, therefore, faith, hope, and charity have their opposing forces. As illustrated in the letter from which I quoted, the antithesis of faith[14] is doubt; the opposite of hope is despair. And the opposite of charity is disregard or even disdain for the Savior and His commandments.

Therefore, in our quest for faith, hope, and charity, we must beware of the dangers of doubt, despair, or disdain for the divine. Moroni so taught: "If ye have no hope ye must needs be in despair; and despair cometh because of iniquity."[15]

Each of us is special, valued, and needed in building the kingdom of God. The adversary is also aware of our worth and will surely taunt us. When Satan's temptations come our way, we need to remember this counsel from Alma: "Humble yourselves before the Lord, and call on his holy name, and watch and pray continually, that ye may not be tempted above that which ye can bear. . . .

"Having faith on the Lord; having a hope that ye shall receive eternal life; having the love of God always in your hearts."[16]

## ANCHOR OF FAITH AND HOPE

A more excellent hope is mightier than a wistful wish. Hope, fortified by faith and charity, forges a force as strong as steel. Hope becomes an anchor to the soul. To this anchor, the faithful can cling, securely tethered to the Lord. Satan, on the other hand, would have us cast away that anchor and drift with the ebb

117

tide of despair. If we will cling to the anchor of hope, it will be our safeguard *forever*.

As declared in scripture: "Wherefore, whoso believeth in God might with surety hope for a better world, yea, even a place at the right hand of God, which hope cometh of faith, maketh an anchor to the souls of men, which would make them sure and steadfast."[17]

The Lord of hope invites all people to come unto Him. Steps toward Him begin with faith, repentance, and baptism. Moroni explained that "the remission of sins bringeth meekness, and lowliness of heart; and . . . the visitation of the Holy Ghost, which Comforter filleth with *hope* and perfect love, . . . until the end shall come, when all the saints shall dwell with God."[18] That destiny can be realized only when we "have faith unto repentance."[19]

Insufficient hope often means insufficient repentance. The Apostle John said that "every man that hath this hope in [God] purifieth himself, even as he is pure."[20]

### THE FRUITS OF FAITH AND HOPE

The fruits of faith and hope are beautiful to behold. Once in Hawaii several years ago, I met with a vice premier of the People's Republic of China who had requested a visit to the Polynesian Cultural Center. The vice premier was accompanied by his wife and by the Chinese ambassador to the United States. More than twenty other dignitaries were also in their party. Because Elder Loren C. Dunn of the Seventy and I were already in Hawaii for meetings with Church leaders, we were asked to go to the center and extend an official welcome to the Chinese delegation in behalf of the First Presidency and General Authorities.

As these influential visitors toured the center and the adjoining BYU—Hawaii Campus, they were impressed. The vice premier noted the sisterly and brotherly blending of some sixty different nationalities and thirty different languages. He even noticed that Samoans sang with Fijians, that Tongans danced with Tahitians, and so on. The spirit of unity among the Latter-day Saint youth was easily evident to all of us.

Finally he asked the question, "How do you promote such unity among your young people?" I answered his question later when I presented a copy of the Book of Mormon to him, describing it as the precious document promoting that unity—and joy.

Regardless of nationality, the Saints have always understood the word of the Lord, who declared: "I say unto you, be one; and if ye are not one ye are not mine."[21]

When the Church's two thousandth stake was created in Mexico City in 1994, President Howard W. Hunter said that the "great purposes of the Lord could not have been achieved with dissension or jealousy or selfishness. . . . [The Lord] will bless each of us as we cast off pride, pray for strength, and contribute to the good of the whole."[22]

In stark contrast to that divine objective, the real world in which we live is divided by diverse languages, culture, and politics. Even the privileges of a democracy carry the burden of bickering in election campaigns. Contention is all about us. Ours is a pessimistic and cynical world—one that, to a great extent, has no hope in Christ or in God's plan for human happiness. Why such global contention and gloom? The reason is plain. If there is no hope in Christ, there is no recognition of a divine plan for the redemption of mankind. Without that knowledge, people mistakenly believe that existence today is followed by extinction tomorrow—that happiness and family associations are only ephemeral.

Such fallacies feed contention. The Book of Mormon bears

record of these words from the first sermon of the Lord Jesus Christ to the people of ancient America: "I say unto you, he that hath the spirit of contention is not if me, but is of the devil, who is the father of contention, and he stirreth up the hearts of men to contend with anger, one with another.

"Behold, this is not my doctrine, to stir up the hearts of men with anger, one against another; but this is my doctrine, that such things should be done away."[23]

## THE IMPORTANCE OF NAMES

Unfortunately, our modern society is caught up in divisive disputation. Often unkind nicknames are added to—or even substituted for—given names. Labels are invented to foster feelings of segregation and competition. For example, athletic teams acquire names to intimidate others, such as "Giants," "Tigers," "Warriors," and so on. Harmless you say? Well, perhaps not overly important. But that is only the beginning. More serious separation results when offensive labels are utilized with the intent to demean.

Even worse, such terms camouflage our true identity as sons and daughters of God. The desire of my heart is that we might rise above such worldly trends. God wants us to ascend to the highest level of our potential. He employs names that unify and sanctify. He gave a new name to Abraham's grandson, Jacob, saying, "Thy name shall be called no more Jacob, but Israel: for as a prince hast thou power with God and with men."[24] In Hebrew, the term *Yisra'el* means "God prevails." Jacob was given a name to match his divine destiny.

When we embrace the gospel and are baptized, we are born again. We take upon ourselves the sacred name of Jesus Christ.[25] We become His sons and daughters and are known as brothers

120

and sisters.[26] We become members of His family; He is the Father of our new life.

In receiving a patriarchal blessing, we each receive a declaration of lineage—a name that links us to our heritage. We understand how we become joint heirs to promises once given by the Lord directly to Abraham, Isaac, and Jacob.[27]

When we know who we are and what God expects of us, we are filled with hope and made aware of our significant role in His great plan of happiness. The day in which we now live was foreseen even *before* Jesus Christ was born, when a prophet said, "Our father hath not spoken of our seed alone, but also of all the house of Israel, pointing to the covenant which should be fulfilled *in the latter days;* which covenant the Lord made to our father Abraham, saying: In thy seed shall all the kindreds of the earth be blessed."[28]

These are those latter days. We are the ones foredetermined and foreordained to fulfill that promise.[29] We are the seed of Abraham, Isaac, and Jacob. We are, in fact, the hope of Israel. We are God's treasure, reserved for our particular place and time.

No wonder China's vice premier noted what he did. Our faithful Latter-day Saints are filled with hope and motivated by love of the Lord Jesus Christ. With that hope, we assiduously avoid labels that could be interpreted as derogatory. When the Nephites were truly righteous, their previous patterns of polarization vanished. "There was no contention in the land, because of the love of God which did dwell in the hearts of the people. . . .

"There were no robbers, nor murderers, neither were there Lamanites, nor any manner of -ites; but they were in one, the children of Christ, and heirs to the kingdom of God.

"And how blessed were they!"[30]

Unfortunately, the sequel to that story is not a happy one. This pleasant circumstance persisted until "a small part of the people . . . had revolted . . . and taken upon them the name of Lamanites,"[31] reviving old prejudices and teaching their children again to hate, "even as the Lamanites were taught to hate the children of Nephi from the beginning."[32] And so the polarizing process began all over again.

I hope that we may learn this important lesson and delete segregating names from our personal vocabularies. The Apostle Paul taught that "there is neither Jew nor Greek, there is neither bond nor free, there is neither male nor female: for ye are all one in Christ Jesus."[33]

Our Savior invites us "to come unto him and partake of his goodness; and he denieth none that come unto him, black and white, bond and free, male and female; . . . all are alike unto God."[34]

## HOPE OF ETERNAL LIFE

Happiness comes when scriptures are used in shaping our lives. They speak of the "brightness of hope"[35] for which we yearn. But if our hopes were narrowly confined only to moments in mortality, we should surely be disappointed. Our ultimate hope must be anchored to the atonement of the Lord Jesus Christ. He said, "If you keep my commandments and endure to the end you shall have eternal life, which gift is the greatest of all the gifts of God."[36]

An understanding of that objective should help us approach the future with faith instead of fear,[37] with a more excellent hope in place of despair. God sent each of us here to be happy and successful.[38] Meanwhile, He also needs us. We are to "seek not the things of this world but seek . . . first to build up the kingdom of God, and to establish his righteousness."[39] He decreed that "no one can assist in this work except he shall be humble and full of love, having faith, hope, and charity, being temperate in all things."[40]

President Howard W. Hunter was such an individual. On one occasion, he said: "It is incumbent upon us to rejoice a little more and despair a little less, to give thanks for what we have and for the magnitude of God's blessings to us. . . .

"For Latter-day Saints this is a time of great hope and excitement—one of the greatest eras . . . of all dispensations. . . . We need to have faith and hope, two of the greatest fundamental virtues of any discipleship of Christ. We must continue to exercise confidence in God. . . . He will bless us as a people. . . . He will bless us as individuals. . . .

"I promise you . . . in the name of the Lord whose servant I am that God will always protect and care for his people. . . . With the gospel of Jesus Christ you have every hope and promise and reassurance. The Lord has power over his Saints and will always prepare places of peace, defense, and safety for his people. When we have faith in God we can hope for a better world—for us personally and for all mankind. . . .

"Disciples of Christ in every generation are invited, indeed commanded, to be filled with a perfect brightness of hope."[41]

President Hunter's counsel is timeless.

By way of summary and promise, I quote the words of Nephi: "Ye must press forward with a steadfastness in Christ, having a perfect brightness of hope, and a love of God and of all men. Wherefore, if ye shall press forward, feasting upon the word of Christ, and endure to the end, behold, thus saith the Father: Ye shall have eternal life."[42]

Our hope is our "Redeemer, the Holy One of Israel—the God of the whole earth."[43] His hope is in us. We are literally the "Hope of Israel, Zion's army, Children of the promised day."[44]

In the words of the Apostle Paul, may "the God of hope fill

[us] with all joy and peace in believing, that [we] may abound in hope, through the power of the Holy Ghost."[45]

May we feast upon the words of Christ and apply His teachings in our lives—that success may attend our righteous endeavors; that health, happiness, and a more excellent hope may be ours; that we may endure to the end and enjoy eternal life.

NOTES

1. Ether 12:32; emphasis added.

2. The writer's name has been withheld to preserve confidentiality. Minor editing has been done to condense the message.

3. D&C 121:45.

4. D&C 63:20.

5. Abraham 3:25.

6. Articles of Faith 1:13; emphasis added.

7. 1 Corinthians 15:19.

8. Moroni 7:41; see also Alma 27:28.

9. Alexander Pope, *An Essay on Man, Epistle 1,* line 95.

10. See 1 Corinthians 13:13, Alma 7:24, Ether 12:28, D&C 4:5.

11. See Moroni 7:47.

12. Moroni 10:20–21; see also Ether 12:9, 34.

13. See 2 Nephi 2:10–11, 15.

14. For descriptions, see Hebrews 11:1, Alma 32:21.

15. Moroni 10:22.

16. Alma 13:28–29.

17. Ether 12:4; see also verse 9 and Hebrews 6:19.

18. Moroni 8:26; emphasis added.

19. Alma 34:15.

20. 1 John 3:3.

21. D&C 38:27.

22. Address delivered at the creation of the Mexico, Mexico City Contreras Stake, 11 December 1994.

23. 3 Nephi 11:29–30.

24. Genesis 32:28.

25. See D&C 20:37.

26. See Mosiah 5:7.

27. See Galatians 3:29; D&C 86:8–11.

28. 1 Nephi 15:18; emphasis added.

29. See Alma 13:3.

30. 4 Nephi 1:15, 17–18.

31. 4 Nephi 1:20.

32. 4 Nephi 1:39.

33. Galatians 3:28; see also Colossians 3:11.

34. 2 Nephi 26:33. Scripture declares that God "made the world and all things therein, . . . [and] hath made of one blood all nations of men for to dwell on all the face of the earth" (Acts 17:24, 26).

35. 2 Nephi 31:20.

36. D&C 14:7. In addition, President Joseph F. Smith said, "The great truth enunciated by the Savior seems very generally to be lost sight of in this generation, that it will profit a man nothing tho' he should gain the whole world if he lose his own soul.

"The standard of success as declared by the word of God, is the salvation of the soul. The greatest gift of God is eternal life" (*Juvenile Instructor,* 15 September 1904, 561–62).

37. See D&C 6:36.

38. See 2 Nephi 2:25, Jacob 2:18–19.

39. JST, Matthew 6:38.

40. D&C 12:8.

41. *BYU 1992–93 Devotional and Fireside* Speeches (Provo: Brigham Young University, 1993), 70–71.

42. 2 Nephi 31:20; see also 2 Nephi 32:3.

43. 3 Nephi 22:5.

44. *Hymns,* 1985, no 259.

45. Romans 15:13.

# ENDURE AND BE LIFTED UP

Early in our married life when Sister Nelson and I lived in Minneapolis, we decided to enjoy a free afternoon with our two-year-old daughter. We went to one of Minnesota's many beautiful lakes and rented a small boat. After rowing far from shore, we stopped to relax and enjoy the tranquil scene. Suddenly, our little toddler lifted one leg out of the boat and started to go overboard, exclaiming, "Time to get out, Daddy!"

Quickly we caught her and explained: "No, dear, it's not time to get out; we must stay in the boat until it brings us safely back to land." Only with considerable persuasion did we succeed in convincing her that leaving the boat early would have led to disaster.

Children are prone to do such dangerous things simply because they have not acquired the wisdom their parents have. Similarly, we as children of our Heavenly Father may foolishly want to get "out of the boat" before we arrive at destinations He would like us to reach. The Lord teaches over and over that we are to endure[1] to the end.[2] This is a dominant theme of the scriptures. One example may serve to represent many passages that convey a similar message:

"Blessed are they who shall seek to bring forth my Zion . . .

126

for they shall have the gift and the power of the Holy Ghost; and if they endure unto the end they shall be lifted up at the last day, and shall be saved in the everlasting kingdom of the Lamb."[3]

Blessings bestowed by God are always predicated upon obedience to law.[4] Applied to my analogy, we are first to get "on the boat" with Him. Then we are to *stay* with Him. And if we don't get "out of the boat" before we should, we shall reach His kingdom, where we will be lifted up to eternal life.

I use a simple demonstration to illustrate that the term "lifted up" relates to a physical law.[5] When I blow into the axial hole of a spool of thread, the force of my breath moves a piece of tissue paper away from me. Next I take an ordinary card and a straight pin. I place the pin through the card. With the pin in the hole of the spool, I hold the card close to the spool. I again blow into the hole of the spool. As I blow, I let go of the card, so that it can respond to physical forces. What do you predict will happen? Will I blow the card away from me, or will the card be lifted up toward me?

As long as I have sufficient breath, the card is lifted up. But when I can endure no longer, the card falls. When my breath gives out, the opposing force of gravity prevails. If my energy could endure, the card would be lifted up indefinitely.[6]

Energy is always required to provide lift over opposing forces. These same laws apply in our personal lives. Whenever an undertaking is begun, both the energy and the will to endure are essential. The winner of a five-kilometer race is declared at the end of *five* kilometers, not at one or two. If you board a bus to Boston, you don't get off at Burlington. If you want to gain an education, you don't drop out along the way—just as you don't pay to dine at an elegant restaurant only to walk away after sampling the salad.

Whatever your work may be, endure at the beginning,

endure through opposing forces along the way, and endure to the end. Any job must be completed before you can enjoy the result for which you are working. So wrote the poet:

> Stick to your task till it sticks to you;
> Beginners are many, but enders are few.
> Honor, power, place, and praise
> Will always come to the one who stays.
> Stick to your task till it sticks to you;
> Bend at it, sweat at it, smile at it too;
> For out of the bend and the sweat and the smile
> Will come life's victories, after awhile.[7]

Sometimes the need to endure comes when facing a physical challenge. Anyone afflicted with a serious illness or with the infirmities of age hopes to be able to endure to the end of such trials.[8] Most often, intense physical challenges are accompanied by spiritual challenges as well.

Think of the early pioneers. What if they had not endured the hardships of their westward migration? Steadfastly they endured—through persecution,[9] expulsion,[10] a governmental order of extermination,[11] expropriation of property,[12] and much more. Their enduring faith in the Lord provided lift for them as it will for you and for me.

The Lord's ultimate concern is for the salvation and exaltation of each individual soul. What if the Apostle Paul's conversion had not been enduring? He never would have testified as he did at the end of his ministry: "I have fought a good fight, I have finished my course, I have kept the faith."[13]

What if Jesus had wavered in His commitment to do His Father's will?[14] His Atonement would not have been accomplished. The dead would not be resurrected. The blessings of immortality and eternal life would not be.[15] But Jesus did

128

endure. During His final hour, Jesus prayed to His Father, saying, "I have glorified thee on the earth: I have *finished* the work which thou gavest me to do."[16]

Early in His mortal ministry, Jesus became concerned about the commitment of His followers. He had just fed the five thousand,[17] then had taught them the doctrines of the kingdom. But some had murmured, "This is an hard saying; who can hear it?"[18] Even after He had fed them, many lacked the faith to endure with Him. He turned to the Twelve and said, "Will ye also go away?"

"Then Simon Peter answered him, Lord . . . thou hast the words of eternal life.

"And we believe and are sure that thou art that Christ, the Son of the living God."[19]

Peter's answer defines the real core of commitment. When we know without a doubt that Jesus is the Christ, we will want to stay with Him. When we are surely converted, the power to endure is ours.

This power to endure is critical in those two most important relationships we enter into in life. One is marriage; the other is membership in the Lord's Church. These are also unique in that they are both covenant—not contractual—relationships.

Marriage—especially temple marriage—and family ties involve covenant relationships. They cannot be regarded casually. With divorce rates escalating throughout the world today, it is apparent that many spouses are failing to endure to the end of their commitments to each other. And some temple marriages fail because a husband forgets that his highest and most important priesthood duty is to honor and sustain his wife.[20] The best thing that a father can do for his children is to "love their mother."[21]

President Gordon B. Hinckley has made a statement that each Latter-day Saint husband should heed: "Magnify your

[wife]," he said, "and in so doing you will magnify your priest-hood."[22] To his profound advice we might couple the timeless counsel of Paul, who said, "Let every one of you . . . love his wife even as himself; and the wife see that she reverence her husband."[23] Enduring love provides enduring lift through life's trials. An enduring marriage results when both husband and wife regard their union as one of the two most important commitments they will ever make.

The other commitment of everlasting consequence is to the Lord.[24] Unfortunately, some souls make a covenant with God—signified by the sacred ordinance of baptism—without a heart-felt commitment to endure with Him. Baptism is an extremely important ordinance. But it is only initiatory. The supreme benefits of membership in the Church can be realized only through the exalting ordinances of the temple. These blessings qualify us for "thrones, kingdoms, principalities, and powers"[25] in the celestial kingdom.

The Lord can readily discern between those with superficial signs of activity and those who are deeply rooted in His Church. This Jesus taught in the parable of the sower. He observed that some "have no root in themselves, and so endure but for a time: afterward, when affliction or persecution ariseth for the word's sake, immediately they are offended."[26]

Loyalty to the Lord carries an obligation of loyalty to those called by the Lord to lead His Church. He has empowered that men be ordained to speak in His holy name.[27] As they guide His unsinkable boat safely toward the shore of salvation, we would do well to stay on board with them.[28] "No waters can swallow the ship where lies / The Master of ocean and earth and skies."[29]

Nevertheless, some individuals want to jump "out of the boat" before reaching land. And others, sadly, are persuaded out by companions who insist that they know more about life's perilous journey than do prophets of the Lord. Problems often arise that are not of your own making. Some of you may innocently find yourselves abandoned by one you trusted. But you will never be forsaken by your Redeemer, who said, "I, the Lord, am bound when ye do what I say."[30]

Without a strong commitment to the Lord, an individual is more prone to have a low level of commitment to a spouse. Weak commitments to eternal covenants lead to losses of eternal consequence. Laments later in life are laced with remorse—as expressed in these lines:

> For of all sad words of tongue or pen,
> The saddest are these: "It might have been!"[31]

We are speaking of the most important of all blessings. The Lord said, "If you keep my commandments and endure to the end you shall have eternal life, which gift is the greatest of all the gifts of God."[32]

Each of you who really wants to endure to the glorious end that our Heavenly Father has foreseen should firmly establish some personal priorities. With many interests competing for your loyalty, you need to be careful first to stay safely "on the boat." No one can serve two masters.[33] If Satan can get you to love anything—fun, flirtation, fame, or fortune—more than a spouse or the Lord with whom you have made sacred covenants to endure, the adversary begins to triumph. When faced with such temptations, you will find that strength comes from commitments made well in advance. The Lord said, "Settle this in your hearts, that ye will do the things which I shall teach, and command you."[34] He declared through His prophet Jeremiah, "I will put my law in their inward parts, and write it in their hearts; and will be their God, and they shall be my people."[35]

When priorities are proper, the power to endure is

increased. And when internalized, those priorities will help keep you from "going overboard." They will protect you from cheating—in marriage, in the Church, and in life.

If you really want to *be* like the Lord—more than any *thing* or any *one* else—you will remember that your adoration of Jesus is best shown by your emulation of Him. Then you will not allow any other love to become more important than love for your companion, your family, and your Creator. You will govern yourself not by someone else's set of rules but by revealed principles of truth.

Your responsibility to endure is uniquely yours. But you are never alone. I testify that the lifting power of the Lord can be yours if you will "come unto Christ" and "be perfected in him." You will "deny yourselves of all ungodliness." And you will "love God with all your might, mind and strength."[36]

The living prophet of the Lord has issued a clarion call: "I invite every one of you," said President Gordon B. Hinckley, "to stand on your feet and with a song in your heart move forward, living the gospel, loving the Lord, and building the kingdom. Together we shall *stay* the course and *keep* the faith."[37]

I pray that each of us may so endure and be lifted up at the last day.

NOTES

1. The word *endure* comes from two Latin roots. The prefix *en* means "within." The remainder comes from the verb *durare,* which means "to be firm or solid." Thus, to *endure* means "to become firm within yourself." That meaning carries into the original languages of the Bible.

In the Hebrew language of the Old Testament, the root word *'aman* means "to render firm" or "to be faithful, to trust." It was often translated as "faithful," but never as "faith" alone. *'Aman* meant more than faith. It was not a passive term; it meant "a firm resolve to be faithful." *'Aman* was also the Hebrew root for words

that were translated into related terms, such as "verified," "believe," "long con-
tinuance," "assurance," "establish(ed)," "sure," "trust," "steadfast," "stand fast," and
others.

In the Greek language of the New Testament, the verb *hupoméno* was used.
It means "to remain," "stay," or "continue." *Hupo* (or *hypo*) means "under," as in
*hypodermic* ("under the skin") or *hypothermia* ("low temperature"). "To endure"
connotes a commitment *within* one's soul.

2. See Matthew 24:13; Mark 13:13; 2 Nephi 33:4; Omni 1:26; 3 Nephi
15:9; D&C 14:7; 18:22; 20:29. This promise has been confirmed by both our
Father in Heaven and the Lord Jesus Christ. From the great Elohim, we have this
pronouncement: "The words of my Beloved are true and faithful. He that
endureth to the end, the same shall be saved" (2 Nephi 31:15). And from the Savior, we have this promise: "Whoso repenteth and is baptized in my name shall be
filled; and if he endureth to the end, . . . him will I hold guiltless before my Father
at that day when I shall stand to judge the world" (3 Nephi 27:16).

3. 1 Nephi 13:37; see also Mosiah 23:22; Alma 13:29; 36:3; 37:37; 38:5; 3
Nephi 27:21–22; Ether 4:19; D&C 5:35; 9:14; 17:8; 75:16. For additional
emphasis, scriptures teach the negative consequences of disobedience to this
commandment. For example, "If they will not repent and believe in his name,
and be baptized in his name, and endure to the end, they must be damned; for
the Lord God, the Holy One of Israel, has spoken it" (2 Nephi 9:24; see also 2
Nephi 31:16; Mormon 9:29).

4. See D&C 130:20–21.

5. This demonstration of Bernoulli's principle in physics was first shown to
the author on 17 August 1996 by Elder Norman C. Boehm, then an Area Authority of the Church residing in Sacramento, California.

6. The law of lift is at work whenever airplanes fly. It is a "component of the
total aerodynamic force acting on an airfoil or on an entire aircraft or winged
missile perpendicular to the relative wind and normally exerted in an upward
direction, opposing the pull of gravity" (*American Heritage Dictionary* [1982], s.v.
"lift").

7. Author unknown, "Stick to Your Task," in *Best-Loved Poems of the LDS*

*People,* ed. Jack M. Lyon and others (Salt Lake City: Deseret Book Co., 1996), 255–56.

8. In his 95th year, President Joseph Fielding Smith publicly expressed the hope that he would be able "to endure to the end in this life" (in Conference Report, October 1970, 92; or *Improvement Era,* December 1970, 27). He who served so faithfully and well all of his days provided a model for all of us to follow.

9. See Joseph Smith—History 1:20, 22–24, 27, 58, 60–61, 74.

10. The pioneers were driven from Ohio to Missouri to Illinois and finally to the valley of the Great Salt Lake.

11. The early pioneers were forced out of Missouri under threat of an order signed by Missouri's governor directing that the "Mormons must be treated as enemies and *must be exterminated* or driven from the state" (*History of the Church,* 7 vols., 2d ed. [Salt Lake City: Deseret Book Co., 1967], 3:175).

12. In 1887, the Congress of the U.S.A. took the unprecedented step of eliminating the Church's legal existence by revoking its corporate charter and authorizing federal receivers to assume ownership of virtually all of the Church's property and other assets, including its most sacred houses of worship— temples—in Logan, Manti, St. George, and Salt Lake City (see *The Late Corporation of The Church of Jesus Christ of Latter-Day Saints v. United States,* 136 U.S. 1 [1890]).

13. 2 Timothy 4:7.

14. See 3 Nephi 27:13.

15. See Moses 1:39.

16. John 17:4; emphasis added. See also John 4:34.

17. See Matthew 14:21; 16:9; Mark 6:44; 8:19; Luke 9:14; John 6:10.

18. John 6:60.

19. John 6:67–69.

20. See D&C 42:22.

21. This statement has been made by many leaders of the Church. For example, see Howard W. Hunter, "Being a Righteous Husband and Father," *Ensign,* November 1994, 50; David O. McKay, as quoted by Gordon B. Hinckley, "Reach Out in Love and Kindness," *Ensign,* November 1982, 77.

22. First session of member fireside conference in Lima, Peru, 9 November 1996.

23. Ephesians 5:33.

24. In addition, worthy men are privileged to qualify for the oath and covenant of the priesthood, which will bless all men, women, and children whom they serve (see D&C 84:33–48).

25. D&C 132:19.

26. Mark 4:17.

27. See D&C 1:38; 21:5; 68:4.

28. See Acts 27:30–31; 1 Nephi 18:21–23.

29. "Master, the Tempest Is Raging," *Hymns,* no. 105.

30. D&C 82:10.

31. John Greenleaf Whittier, "Maud Muller," *The Complete Poetical Works of Whittier* (1892), 48.

32. D&C 14:7. The Prophet Joseph included this concept of endurance in the thirteenth article of faith: "We have endured many things, and hope to be able to endure all things."

33. See Matthew 6:24.

34. JST, Luke 14:28.

35. Jeremiah 31:33.

36. Moroni 10:32.

37. "Stay the Course—Keep the Faith," *Ensign,* November 1995, 72; emphasis added.

# DOORS OF DEATH

$A$ t the funeral of a friend, I visited with two distinguished brothers—former surgical colleagues of mine—whose lovely companions had both passed away. They said they were going through the most difficult period of their lives, adjusting to the almost unbearable loss of their partners. These wonderful men then told of their cooking breakfast for each other once a week, sharing that rotation with their sister, trying to lessen their loneliness imposed by the doors of death.

Death separates "the spirit and the body [which] are the soul of man."[1] That separation evokes pangs of sorrow and shock among those left behind. The hurt is real. Only its intensity varies. Some doors are heavier than others. The sense of tragedy may be related to age. Generally, the younger the victim, the greater the grief. Yet even when the elderly or infirm have been afforded merciful relief, their loved ones are rarely ready to let go. The only length of life that seems to satisfy the longings of the human heart is life everlasting.

## MOURNING

Irrespective of age, we mourn for those loved and lost.

Mourning is one of the deepest expressions of pure love. It is a natural response in complete accord with divine commandment: "Thou shalt live together in love, insomuch that thou shalt weep for the loss of them that die."[2]

Moreover, we can't fully appreciate joyful reunions later without tearful separations now. The only way to take sorrow out of death is to take love out of life.

## Eternal Perspective

Eternal perspective provides peace "which passeth all understanding."[3] In speaking at a funeral of a loved one, the Prophet Joseph Smith offered this admonition: "When we lose a near and dear friend, upon whom we have set our hearts, it should be a caution unto us. . . . Our affections should be placed upon God and His work, more intensely than upon our fellow beings."[4]

Life does not begin with birth, nor does it end with death. Prior to our birth, we dwelled as spirit children with our Father in Heaven. There we eagerly anticipated the possibility of coming to earth and obtaining a physical body. Knowingly we wanted the risks of mortality, which would allow the exercise of agency and accountability. "This life [was to become] a probationary state; a time to prepare to meet God."[5] But we regarded the returning home as the best part of that long-awaited trip, just as we do now. Before embarking on any journey, we like to have some assurance of a round-trip ticket. Returning from earth to life in our heavenly home requires passage through—and not around—the doors of death. We were born to die, and we die to live.[6] As seedlings of God, we barely blossom on earth; we fully flower in heaven.

137

## PHYSICAL DEATH

The writer of Ecclesiastes said, "To every thing there is a season, and a time to every purpose under the heaven:

"A time to be born, and a time to die."[7]

Think of the alternative. If all 69 billion people who have ever lived on earth were still here, imagine the traffic jam! And we could own virtually nothing and scarcely make any responsible decisions.

## PLAN OF HAPPINESS

Scriptures teach that death is *essential* to happiness: "Now behold, it was not expedient that man should be reclaimed from this temporal death, for that would *destroy* the great plan of happiness."[8]

Our limited perspective would be enlarged if we could witness the reunion on the other side of the veil, when doors of death open to those returning home. Such was the vision of the psalmist who wrote, "Precious in the sight of the Lord is the death of his saints."[9]

## SPIRITUAL DEATH

But there is another type of separation known in scripture as spiritual death."[10] It "is defined as a state of spiritual alienation from God."[11] Thus, one can be very much alive physically but dead spiritually.

Spiritual death is more likely when goals are unbalanced toward things physical. Paul explained this concept to the Romans: "If ye live after the flesh, ye shall die: but if ye through the Spirit do mortify the deeds of the body, ye shall live."[12]

If physical death should strike before moral wrongs have

been made right, opportunity for repentance will have been forfeited. Thus, "the [real] sting of death is sin."[13]

Even the Savior cannot save us in our sins. He will redeem us from our sins, but only upon condition of our repentance. We are responsible for our own spiritual survival or death.[14]

## COPING WITH TRIALS

Physical and spiritual trials provide continuing challenges in life. Those who are at the twilight of life endure long and difficult days. They know well the meaning of that divine injunction to "endure to the end."[15]

The Savior of the world repeatedly asked that we pattern our lives after His.[16] So we must endure trials—as did He. "Though he were a Son, yet learned he obedience by the things which he suffered."[17]

When hardship heaps its heavy load upon us, good may yet be gleaned. Shakespeare so wrote:

> Sweet are the uses of adversity,
> Which, like the toad, ugly and venomous,
> Wears yet a precious jewel in his head.[18]

The Lord's expression is even more explicit: "After much tribulation come the blessings."[19]

## POSTMORTAL LIFE

Mortality, temporary as it is, is terminated by the doors of death. Questions then come to searching minds of those left behind: "Where is my loved one now?" "What happens after death?" While many questions cannot be fully answered with available knowledge, much is known.

## PARADISE

The first station in postmortal life is named paradise. Alma wrote: "Concerning the state of the soul between death and the resurrection—Behold, it has been made known unto me . . . that the spirits of all men, as soon as they are departed from this mortal body, . . . are taken home to that God who gave them life. . . .

"The spirits of those who are righteous are received into a state of happiness, which is called paradise, a state of rest, a state of peace."[20]

## RESURRECTION AND IMMORTALITY

Some facetiously state that nothing is as permanent as death. Not so! The grip of physical death is temporary. It began with the fall of Adam; it ended with the atonement of Jesus the Christ. The waiting period in paradise is temporary, too. It ends with the Resurrection. From the Book of Mormon we learn that the "paradise of God must deliver up the spirits of the righteous, and the grave deliver up the body of the righteous; and the spirit and the body is restored to itself again, and all men become incorruptible, and immortal, and they are living souls."[21]

A few years ago our stake president and his wife had a wonderful son taken in his youthful prime because of an automobile accident. We are consoled by the knowledge that the very laws that could not allow his broken body to survive here are the same eternal laws which the Lord will employ at the time of the Resurrection, when that body "shall be restored to [its] proper and perfect frame."[22]

The Lord who created us in the first place surely has power to do it again. The same necessary elements now in our bodies will still be available—at His command. The same unique genetic code now embedded in each of our living cells will still be

140

available to format new ones then. The miracle of the Resurrection, wondrous as it will be, is marvelously matched by the
miracle of our creation in the first place.

## JUDGMENT

Our resurrection will not be an end but a new beginning. It
will prepare us for judgment by the Lord, who said, "As I have
been lifted up [upon the cross] by men even so should men be
lifted up by the Father, to stand before me, to be judged of their
works."[23]

Even before we approach that threshold of the eternal court
of justice, we know who will personally preside: "The keeper of
the gate is the Holy One of Israel; and he employeth no servant
there; and there is none other way save it be by the gate; for he
cannot be deceived, for the Lord God is his name.

"And whoso knocketh, to him will he open."[24]

## FAMILY TIES

Loving relationships continue beyond the doors of death and
judgment. Family ties endure because of sealing in the temple.
Their importance cannot be overstated.

I remember vividly an experience I had as a passenger in a
small two-propeller airplane. One of its engines suddenly burst
open and caught on fire. The propeller of the flaming engine was
starkly stilled. As we plummeted in a steep spiral dive toward the
earth, I expected to die. Some of the passengers screamed in hys-
terical panic. Miraculously, the precipitous dive extinguished the
flames. Then, by starting up the other engine, the pilot was able
to stabilize the plane and bring us down safely.

Throughout that ordeal, though I "knew" death was coming,
my paramount feeling was that I was not afraid to die. I remember

a sense of returning home to meet ancestors for whom I had done temple work. I remember my deep sense of gratitude that my sweetheart and I had been sealed eternally to each other and to our children, born and reared in the covenant. I realized that our marriage in the temple was my most important accomplishment. Honors bestowed upon me by men could not approach the inner peace provided by sealings performed in the house of the Lord.

That harrowing experience consumed but a few minutes, yet my entire life flashed before my mind. Having had such rapid recall when facing death, I do not doubt the scriptural promise of "perfect remembrance" facing judgment.[25]

## ETERNAL LIFE

After judgment comes the possibility of eternal life—the kind of life that our Heavenly Father lives. His celestial realm has been compared with the glory of the sun.[26] It is available to all who prepare for it, the requirements of which have been clearly revealed: "Ye must press forward with a steadfastness in Christ, having a perfect brightness of hope, and a love of God and of all men. Wherefore, if ye shall press forward, feasting upon the word of Christ, and endure to the end, behold, thus saith the Father: Ye shall have eternal life."[27]

## TIME TO PREPARE

Meanwhile, we who tarry here have a few precious moments remaining "to prepare to meet God."[28] Unfinished business is our worst business. Perpetual procrastination must yield to perceptive preparation. Today we have a little more time to bless others—time to be kinder, more compassionate, quicker to thank and slower to scold, more generous in sharing, more gracious in caring.

Then when our turn comes to pass through the doors of death, we can say as did Paul: "The time of my departure is at hand. I have fought a good fight, I have finished my course, I have kept the faith."[29]

We need not look upon death as an enemy. With our full understanding and preparation, faith supplants fear. Hope displaces despair. The Lord said, "Fear not even unto death; for in this world your joy is not full, but in me your joy is full."[30] He bestowed this gift: "Peace I leave with you, my peace I give unto you: not as the world giveth, give I unto you. Let not your heart be troubled, neither let it be afraid."[31]

As a special witness of Jesus Christ, I testify that He lives! I also testify that the veil of death is very thin. I know by experiences too sacred to relate that those who have gone before are not strangers to leaders of this Church. To us and to you, our loved ones may be just as close as the next room—separated only by the doors of death.

With that assurance, brothers and sisters, love life! Cherish each moment as a blessing from God.[32] Live it well—even to your loftiest potential. Then the anticipation of death shall not hold you hostage. With the help of the Lord, your deeds and desires will qualify you to receive everlasting joy, glory, immortality, and eternal lives.

NOTES

1. D&C 88:15.
2. D&C 42:45.
3. Philippians 4:7.
4. *Teachings of the Prophet Joseph Smith,* 216.
5. Alma 12:24.
6. See 2 Corinthians 6:9.
7. Ecclesiastes 3:1–2; see also Alma 12:27.

8. Alma 42:8; emphasis added. See also 2 Nephi 9:6.

9. Psalm 116:15.

10. See 2 Nephi 9:12; Alma 12:16; 42:9; Helaman 14:16, 18.

11. Joseph Fielding Smith, *Doctrines of Salvation,* 2:217.

12. Romans 8:13.

13. 1 Corinthians 15:56.

14. See Romans 8:13–14; Helaman 14:18; D&C 29:41–45.

15. See Matthew 24:13; Mark 13:13; 1 Nephi 13:37; 22:31; 2 Nephi 31:16; 33:4; Omni 1:26; 3 Nephi 15:9; D&C 14:7; 18:22; 24:8.

16. See John 13:15; 14:6; 1 Peter 2:21; 2 Nephi 31:9, 16; 3 Nephi 18:16; 27:27.

17. Hebrews 5:8.

18. *As You Like It,* act 2, scene 1, lines 12–14.

19. D&C 58:4.

20. Alma 40:11–12.

21. 2 Nephi 9:13.

22. Alma 40:23; see also 11:42–45.

23. 3 Nephi 27:14.

24. 2 Nephi 9:41–42.

25. Alma 5:18; see also Alma 11:43.

26. See 1 Corinthians 15:41; D&C 76:96.

27. 2 Nephi 31:20; see also John 17:3.

28. Alma 34:32.

29. 2 Timothy 4:6–7.

30. D&C 101:36.

31. John 14:27.

32. See Mosiah 2:21.

# PART 3

# CHRIST AND THE COVENANT

# JESUS THE CHRIST— OUR MASTER AND MORE

M y lifelong interest in the human heart took an unexpected turn in April 1984, when I was called to leave the operating room of the hospital and enter the upper room of the temple. There I became an ordained Apostle of the Lord Jesus Christ. I did not seek such a call but have humbly tried to be worthy of that trust and of the privilege of being His representative, now hoping to mend hearts spiritually as I previously did surgically.

As one who has been called, sustained, and ordained—one of the twelve special witnesses of our Lord and Master—I desire to follow a vital theme from the Book of Mormon: "We talk of Christ, we rejoice in Christ, we preach of Christ, [and] we prophesy of Christ."[1]

We honor Him as the most important individual ever to live on planet earth. He is Jesus the Christ—our Master and more. He has numerous names, titles, and responsibilities, all of eternal significance.[2] Under the heading "Jesus Christ," the Topical Guide in the King James Version of the LDS edition of the Holy Bible has eighteen pages (pages 240–58) filled with references listed under fifty-seven subheadings. We cannot fully consider or comprehend all of these important facets of His life. But I would like to review, even briefly, ten of those mighty responsibilities of Jesus the Christ. I do not want to imply any order of priority— because all that He accomplished was equally supernal in scope.

### CREATOR

Under the direction of the Father, Jesus bore the responsibility of Creator. His title was the *Word*—spelled with a capital W. In the Greek language of the New Testament, that *Word* was *Logos,* or "divine expression." It was another name for the Master. That terminology may seem strange, but it is so reasonable. We use words to convey our expression to others. So Jesus was the "Word" or "Expression" of His Father to the world. The gospel of John begins with this important proclamation:

"In the beginning was the Word, and the Word was with God. . . .

"The same was in the beginning with God.

"All things were made by him; and without him was not any thing made that was made."[3]

The book of Helaman records similar testimony declaring that "Jesus Christ [is] . . . the Creator of all things from the beginning."[4]

Another clarifying quotation comes from Moses: "The Lord God said unto Moses: For mine own purpose have I made these things. . . .

"And by the word of my power, have I created them, which is mine Only Begotten Son, who is full of grace and truth.

"And worlds without number have I created; and I also created them for mine own purpose; and by the Son I created them, which is mine Only Begotten."[5]

148

In modern revelation, Jesus' responsibility as Creator of many worlds is again affirmed:

"Therefore, in the beginning the Word was, for he was the Word, even the messenger of salvation—

"The light and the Redeemer of the world; the Spirit of truth, who came into the world, because the world was made by him, and in him was the life of men and the light of men.

"The worlds were made by him; men were made by him; all things were made by him, and through him, and of him."[6]

This hallowed Creator provided that each of us could have a physical body, uniquely individual, yet in many respects comparable to every other human body. Just as a well-educated musician can recognize the composer of a symphony by its style and structure, so a well-educated surgeon can recognize the Creator of human beings by the similarity and style and structure of our anatomy. Individual variations notwithstanding, this similarity provides additional evidence and deep spiritual confirmation of our divine creation by our same Creator. It enhances the understanding of our relationship to Him:

"The Gods went down to organize man in their own image, in the image of the Gods to form they him, male and female to form they them.

"And the Gods said: We will bless them."[7]

Indeed, they have blessed each of us. Our bodies can repair and defend themselves. They regenerate new cells to replace old ones. Our bodies carry seeds that allow reproduction of our own kind with our unique individual characteristics. Little wonder our Creator is also known as the Great Physician[8]—able to heal the sick,[9] restore sight to the blind,[10] unstop ears of the deaf,[11] and raise the dead.[12] And in these latter days, He has revealed a code of health known as the Word of Wisdom that has blessed the lives of all who have obeyed those teachings in faith. So we honor Jesus our Creator, divinely directed by His Father.

## JEHOVAH

Jesus was Jehovah. This sacred title is recorded only four times in the King James version of the Holy Bible.[13] The use of this holy name is also confirmed in modern scripture.[14] *Jehovah* is derived from the Hebrew word *hayah,* which means "to be" or "to exist." A form of the word *hayah* in the Hebrew text of the Old Testament was translated into English as "I AM."[15] Remarkably, *I AM* was used by Jehovah as a name for Himself.[16] Listen to this intriguing dialogue from the Old Testament. Moses had just received a divine appointment that He did not seek—a commission to lead the children to Israel out of bondage. The scene takes place atop Mount Sinai:

"Moses said unto God, Who am I, that I should go unto Pharaoh, and that I should bring forth the children of Israel out of Egypt? . . . [No doubt Moses felt inadequate for his calling, even as you and I may feel when given a challenging assignment.]

"And Moses said unto God, Behold, when I come unto the children of Israel, and shall say unto them, The God of your fathers hath sent me unto you; and they shall say to me, What is his name? what shall I say unto them?

"And God said unto Moses, I AM THAT I AM: and he said, Thus shalt thou say unto the children of Israel, I AM hath sent me unto you.

"And God said moreover unto Moses, Thus shalt thou say unto the children of Israel, The Lord God of your fathers, the God of Abraham, the God of Isaac, and the God of Jacob, hath sent me unto you: this is my name for ever."[17]

Jehovah had thus revealed to Moses this very name that He

had meekly and modestly chosen for His own premortal identification—I AM.

Later, in His mortal ministry, Jesus occasionally repeated His name. Do you remember His terse response to tormenting questioners? Note the double meaning in His reply:

"The high priest asked him, . . . Art thou the Christ, the Son of the Blessed?

"And Jesus said, I am."[18]

He was declaring both His lineage and His name.

Another instance occurred when Jesus was taunted about His acquaintanceship with Abraham:

"Then said the Jews unto him, . . . hast thou seen Abraham?

"Jesus said unto them, Verily, verily, I say unto you, Before Abraham was, I am."[19]

Jehovah—the Great I AM, God of the Old Testament—clearly identified Himself when the resurrected Jesus personally appeared in His glory to the Prophet Joseph Smith and Oliver Cowdery in the Kirtland Temple on 3 April 1836. I quote from their written testimony:

"We saw the Lord standing upon the breastwork of the pulpit, before us; and under his feet was a paved work of pure gold, in color like amber.

"His eyes were as a flame of fire; the hair of his head was white like the pure snow; his countenance shone above the brightness of the sun; and his voice was as the sound of the rushing of great waters, even the voice of Jehovah, saying:

"*I am* the first and the last; *I am* he who liveth, *I am* he who was slain."[20]

Jesus fulfilled His responsibility as Jehovah, "the Great I AM," with eternal consequence.

## ADVOCATE WITH THE FATHER

Jesus is our Advocate with the Father.[21] The word *advocate* comes from Latin roots meaning a "voice for," or "one who pleads for another." Other related terms are used in scripture, such as *intercessor* or *mediator*.[22] From the Book of Mormon we learn that this responsibility was foreseen before His birth:

"[Jesus] shall make intercession for all the children of men; and they that believe in him shall be saved."[23]

This mission was clearly evident in the compassionate intercessory prayer of Jesus. Picture Him in your mind, kneeling in fervent supplication. Listen to the beautiful language of His prayer. Sense His feeling for His weighty responsibility as mediator:

"I have manifested thy name unto the men which thou gavest me out of the world: thine they were, and thou gavest them me; and they have kept thy word.

"Now they have known that all things whatsoever thou hast given me are of thee.

"For I have given unto them the words which thou gavest me; and they have received them, and have known surely that I came out from thee, and they have believed that thou didst send me.

"I pray for them."[24]

He is also known as the mediator of the new testament or covenant.[25] Comprehending Him as our advocate-intercessor-mediator with the Father gives us assurance of His unequaled understanding, justice, and mercy.[26]

## IMMANUEL

Jesus was foreordained to be the promised Immanuel. Remember Isaiah's remarkable prophecy:

152

"The Lord himself shall give you a sign; Behold, a virgin shall conceive, and bear a son, and shall call his name Immanuel."[27]

Fulfillment of that prophecy was not just unlikely—it was humanly impossible! Incredible! Everyone knew that a virgin could not bear a child. And then for that child to be given such a pretentious name was doubly daring! The Hebrew name that Isaiah announced—*Immanuel*—literally means "with us [is] God!"

That holy name was subsequently given to Jesus in the New Testament, the Book of Mormon, and the Doctrine and Covenants.[28]

Immanuel could be such only at the will of His Father.

## SON OF GOD

Jesus alone bore His responsibility as the Son of God—the Only Begotten Son of the Father.[29] Jesus was literally "the Son of the Highest."[30] In more than a dozen verses of scripture, the solemn word of God the Father bears testimony that Jesus was truly His Beloved Son. That solemn testimony was often coupled with God's pleading for mankind to hear and obey the voice of His revered Son.[31] Through the condescension of God, that most unlikely prophecy of Isaiah had become reality.

The unique parentage of Jesus was also announced to Nephi, who was thus instructed by an angel:

"Behold, the virgin whom thou seest is the mother of the Son of God, after the manner of the flesh. . . .

" . . . Behold the Lamb of God, yea, even the Son of the Eternal Father!"[32]

From His mother, Jesus inherited His potential for mortality and death.[33] From His Heavenly Father, Jesus inherited His potential for immortality and eternal life. Prior to His crucifixion, He spoke these words of clarification: "I lay down my life, that I might take it again.

153

"No man taketh it from me, but I lay it down of myself. I have power to lay it down, and I have power to take it again. This . . . have I received of my Father."[34]

Though separate from His Heavenly Father in both body and spirit, Jesus is one with His Father in power and purpose. Their ultimate objective is "to bring to pass the immortality and eternal life of man."[35]

Some may wonder why the Son is occasionally referred to as "the Father." The designation used for any man can vary. Every man is a son but may also be called "father," "brother," "uncle," or "grandfather," depending on conversational circumstance. So we must not allow ourselves to become confused regarding divine identity, purpose, or doctrine. Because Jesus was our Creator, He is known in scripture as "the Father of all things."[36] But please remember, "Jesus Christ is not the Father of the spirits who have taken or yet shall take bodies upon this earth, for He is one of them. He is The Son, as they are sons and daughters of Elohim."[37]

We comprehend that distinction well when we pray to our Heavenly Father in the name of His Son, Jesus Christ, through the power of the Holy Ghost. And as we do so regularly, we honor our heavenly and earthly parentage, just as Jesus honored His as the Son of God.

## ANOINTED ONE

"God anointed Jesus of Nazareth with the Holy Ghost and with power."[38] So Jesus was the Anointed One. The Hebrew word for *anointed* is *Messiah,* and the Greek translation is *Christ.* Thus, "Jesus is spoken of as the Christ and the Messiah, which means he is the one anointed of the Father to be his personal representative in all things pertaining to the salvation of mankind."[39] Scriptures declare that *Christ* is the only name under heaven whereby salvation comes.[40] So you may add either of these titles to signify your adoration for Jesus—as "the Christ" or as "the Messiah," anointed by God for that supernal responsibility.

## SAVIOR AND REDEEMER

Jesus was born to be Savior and Redeemer of all mankind.[41] He was the Lamb of God,[42] who offered Himself without spot or blemish[43] as a sacrifice for the sins of the world.[44] Later, as the resurrected Lord, He related that sacred responsibility to the meaning of *the gospel,* which He described in one powerful passage:

"Behold I have given unto you my gospel, and this is the gospel which I have given unto you—that I came into the world to do the will of my Father, because my Father sent me.

"And my Father sent me that I might be lifted up upon the cross."[45]

Thus Jesus personally defined *the gospel.* This term comes from the Old English *godspell,* which literally means "good news."

"The good news is that Jesus Christ has made a perfect atonement for mankind that will redeem all mankind from the grave and reward each individual according to his/her works. This atonement was begun by his appointment in the premortal world but was worked out by Jesus during his mortal sojourn."[46]

His atonement had been foretold long before Jesus was born in Bethlehem. Prophets had so prophesied His advent for many generations. Let us sample from the book of Helaman, written some thirty years before the Savior's birth:

"Remember that there is no other way nor means whereby man can be saved, only through the atoning blood of Jesus Christ, who shall come; yea, remember that he cometh to redeem the world."[47]

His atonement blesses each of us in a very personal way. Listen carefully to this explanation from Jesus:

155

"For behold, I, God, have suffered these things for all, that they might not suffer if they would repent;

"But if they would not repent they must suffer even as I;

"Which suffering caused myself, even God, the greatest of all, to tremble because of pain, and to bleed at every pore, and to suffer both body and spirit—and would that I might not drink the bitter cup, and shrink—

"Nevertheless, glory be to the Father, and I partook and finished my preparations unto the children of men."[48]

Jesus fulfilled His glorious promise made in pre-earthly councils by atoning for the fall of Adam and Eve unconditionally and for our sins upon the condition of our repentance.

His responsibility as Savior and Redeemer was indelibly intertwined with His responsibility as Creator. To shed additional insight on this relationship, I would like to share a remarkable quotation that I found in a rare book in London one day while searching through the library of the British Museum. It was published as a twentieth-century English translation of an ancient Coptic text. It was written by Timothy, Patriarch of Alexandria, who died in A.D. 385. This record refers to the creation of Adam. Premortal Jesus is speaking of His Father:

"He . . . made Adam according to Our image and likeness, and He left him lying for forty days and forty nights without putting breath into him. And He heaved sighs over him daily, saying, 'If I put breath into this [man], he must suffer many pains.' And I said unto My Father, 'Put breath into him; I will be an advocate for him.' And My Father said unto Me, 'If I put breath into him, My beloved Son, Thou wilt be obliged to go down into the world, and to suffer many pains for him before Thou shalt have redeemed him, and made him to come back to his primal state.' And I said unto My Father, 'Put breath into him; I will be his advocate, and I will go down into the world, and will fulfil Thy command.'"[49]

Jesus' responsibility as Advocate, Savior, and Redeemer was foredetermined in premortal realms and fulfilled by His atonement.[50] Your responsibility is to remember, to repent, and to be righteous.

## JUDGE

Closely allied to the Lord's status as Savior and Redeemer is His responsibility as Judge. Jesus revealed this interrelationship after He had declared His definition of *the gospel*, which we just cited:

"As I have been lifted up [upon the cross] by men even so should men be lifted up by the Father, to stand before me, to be judged of their works, whether they be good or whether they be evil—

" . . . Therefore, according to the power of the Father I will draw all men unto me, that they may be judged according to their works."[51]

The Book of Mormon sheds further light on how that judgment will occur. So does the temple endowment. When we approach the threshold of the eternal court of justice, we know who will personally preside:

"The keeper of the gate is the Holy One of Israel; and he employeth no servant there; and there is none other way save it be by the gate; for he cannot be deceived, for the Lord God is his name.

"And whoso knocketh, to him will he open."[52]

Scriptures indicate that the Lord will receive apostolic assistance when exercising judgment upon the house of Israel.[53] Your personal encounter at judgment will be aided by your own "bright recollection"[54] and "perfect remembrance"[55] of your deeds, as well as by the desires of your heart.[56]

## EXEMPLAR

Another responsibility of the Lord is that of Exemplar. To the people of the Holy Land, He said, "I have given you an example, that ye should do as I have done."[57]

To the people of ancient America, He again emphasized His mission as Exemplar: "I am the light; I have set an example for you."[58]

In His Sermon on the Mount, Jesus challenged His followers with this admonition: "Be ye therefore perfect, even as your Father which is in heaven is perfect."[59]

Sinless and flawless as Jesus was in mortality, we should remember that He viewed His own state of physical perfection as being yet in the future.[60] Even He had to endure to the end. Can you and I be expected to do any less?

When the crucified and resurrected Lord appeared to the people in ancient America, He again stressed the importance of His example. But now He included Himself as a perfected personage: "I would that ye should be perfect even as I, or your Father who is in heaven is perfect."[61]

Are you vexed by your own imperfections? Please do not be discouraged by the Lord's expression of hope for your perfection. You should have faith to know that He would not require development beyond your capacity.

Of course you should strive to correct habits or thoughts that are improper. Conquering weakness brings great joy! You can attain a certain degree of perfection in some things in this life. And you can become perfect in keeping various commandments. But the Lord was not necessarily asking for your errorless and perfect behavior in all things. He was pleading for more than that. His hopes are for your full potential to be realized—to become as He is! That includes the perfection of your physical body, when it will be changed to an immortal state that cannot deteriorate or die.

So while you earnestly strive for continuing improvement in your life here, remember your resurrection, exaltation, and perfection await you in the life to come. That precious promise of perfection could not have been possible without the Lord's atonement and His example.

## MILLENNIAL MESSIAH

The Lord's ultimate responsibility lies yet in the future—His masterful status as the Millennial Messiah. When that day comes, the physical face of the earth will have been changed:

"Every valley shall be exalted, and every mountain and hill shall be made low: and the crooked shall be made straight, and the rough places plain."[62]

Then Jesus will return to the earth. His second coming will be no secret. It will be broadly known.

"The glory of the Lord shall be revealed, and all flesh shall see it together."[63]

Then, "the government shall be upon his shoulder: and his name shall be called Wonderful, Counsellor, The mighty God, The everlasting Father, The Prince of Peace."[64] He will govern from two world capitals—one in old Jerusalem[65] and the other in the New Jerusalem "built upon the American continent."[66] From these centers He will direct the affairs of His church and kingdom. Then He "shall reign for ever and ever." [67]

In that day He will bear new titles and be surrounded by special Saints. He will be known as "Lord of lords, and King of kings: and they that [will be] with him [will be those who] are called, and chosen, and faithful" to their trust here in mortality.[68]

He is Jesus the Christ—our Master and more. We have discussed but ten of His many responsibilities: Creator, Jehovah, Advocate with the Father, Immanuel, Son of God, Anointed One, Savior and Redeemer, Judge, Exemplar, and Millennial Messiah.

As His disciples, you and I bear mighty responsibilities, too. In my lifetime I have visited all fifty states in the United States of America. I have also set foot upon the soil of 107 other countries of the earth. Wherever I walk, it is my divine calling and sacred privilege to bear fervent testimony of Jesus the Christ. He lives! I love Him. Eagerly I follow Him, and willingly I offer my life in His service. As His special witness, I solemnly teach of Him. I testify of Him.

NOTES

1. 2 Nephi 25:26.

2. For example, see Daniel H. Ludlow, "Jesus Christ Is Basis of LDS Beliefs," *Church News,* 29 March 1980.

3. John 1:1–3; see also D&C 93:21.

4. Helaman 14:12.

5. Moses 1:31–33.

6. D&C 93:8–10; see also Hebrews 1:2; 1 Corinthians 8:6; 2 Nephi 9:5; 3 Nephi 9:15; D&C 76:23–24; 88:42–48; 101:32–34.

7. Abraham 4:27–28.

8. See Matthew 9:12.

9. See 3 Nephi 9:13; D&C 35:9; 42:48–51.

10. See John 9:1–11.

11. See Isaiah 35:5; 3 Nephi 26:15.

12. See Matthew 9:23–26; John 11:5–45.

13. See Exodus 6:3; Psalm 83:18; Isaiah 12:2; 26:4.

14. See Moroni 10:34; D&C 109:68; 110:3; 128:9.

15. Exodus 3:14.

16. For example, see D&C 29:1; 38:1; 39:1.

17. Exodus 3:11, 13–15.

18. Mark 14:61–62.

19. John 8:57–58.

20. D&C 110:2–4; emphasis added. See also D&C 76:23.

21. See 1 John 2:1; D&C 29:5; 32:3; 45:3; 110:4.

22. See also 1 Timothy 2:5; 2 Nephi 2:28, D&C 76:69.

23. 2 Nephi 2:9.

24. John 17:6–9.

25. See Hebrews 9:15; 12:24.

26. See Alma 7:12.

27. Isaiah 7:14.

28. See Matthew 1:23; 2 Nephi 17:14; D&C 128:22.

29. See John 1:14, 18, 3:16.

30. Luke 1:32, 35.

31. See Matthew 3:17; 17:5; Mark 1:11, 9:7; Luke 3:22; 9:35; 2 Peter 1:17; 2 Nephi 31:11; 3 Nephi 11:7; 21:20; D&C 93:15; Moses 4:2; Joseph Smith—History 1:17.

32. 1 Nephi 11:18, 21.

33. See Genesis 3:15; Mark 6:3.

34. John 10:17–18.

35. Moses 1:39.

36. Mosiah 7:27; see also Mosiah 15:3; 16:15; Helaman 14:12; Ether 3:14.

37. Statement of the First Presidency and the Council of the Twelve Apostles, 30 June 1916, in James E. Talmage, *The Articles of Faith,* appendix 2, 473.

38. Acts 10:38.

39. LDS Bible Dictionary, "Anointed One," 609.

40. See 2 Nephi 25:20.

41. See Isaiah 49:26; 1 Nephi 10:5.

42. See 1 Nephi 10:10.

43. See 1 Peter 1:19.

44. See John 1:29.

45. 3 Nephi 27:13–14.

46. LDS Bible Dictionary, "Gospels," 682.

47. Helaman 5:9.

48. D&C 19:16–19.

49. "Discourse on Abbatôn by Timothy, Archbishop of Alexandria," *Coptic Martyrdoms Etc. in the Dialect of Upper Egypt,* vol. 4 of *Coptic Texts,* edited, with English translations, by E.A. Wallis Budge (London: British Museum, 1914; New York: AMS Press, 1977), 482; brackets appear in printed text. For comparison with related scriptures see Moses 3:7; 6:8–9, 22, 29.

50. See Job 19:25–26; Matthew 1:21.

51. 3 Nephi 27:14–15.

52. 2 Nephi 9:41–42.

53. See 1 Nephi 12:9; D&C 29:12.

54. Alma 11:43.

55. Alma 5:18.

56. See D&C 137:9.

57. John 13:15; see also 14:6; 1 Peter 2:21.

58. 3 Nephi 18:16, see also 27:27; 2 Nephi 31:9, 16.

59. Matthew 5:48.

60. See Luke 13:32.

61. 3 Nephi 12:48.

62. Isaiah 40:4.

63. Isaiah 40:5.

64. Isaiah 9:6.

65. See Zechariah 14:4–7; D&C 45:48–66; 133:19–21.

66. Articles of Faith 1:10; see also Ether 13:3–10; D&C 84:2–4.

67. Revelation 11:15; see also Exodus 15:18; Psalm 146:10; Mosiah 3:5; D&C 76:108.

68. Revelation 17:14; see also 19:16.

# THE ATONEMENT

Humbly I join the Book of Mormon prophet Jacob, who asked, "Why not speak of the atonement of Christ?"[1] This topic comprises our third article of faith: "We believe that through the Atonement of Christ, all mankind may be saved, by obedience to the laws and ordinances of the gospel."

Before we can comprehend the Atonement of Christ, however, we must first understand the Fall of Adam. And before we can understand the Fall of Adam, we must first understand the Creation. These three crucial components of the plan of salvation relate to each other.[2]

## THE CREATION

The Creation culminated with Adam and Eve in the Garden of Eden. They were created in the image of God, with bodies of flesh and bone.[3] Created in the image of God and not yet mortal, they could not grow old and die.[4] "And they would have had no children,"[5] nor experience the trials of life. (Please forgive me for mentioning children and the trials of life in the same breath!) The creation of Adam and Eve was a *paradisiacal creation,* one that required a significant change before they could fulfill the commandment to have children[6] and thus provide earthly bodies for premortal spirit sons and daughters of God.

## THE FALL

That brings us to the Fall. Scripture teaches that "Adam fell that men might be; and men are, that they might have joy."[7] The Fall of Adam and Eve constituted the *mortal creation* and brought about required changes in their bodies, including the circulation of blood and other modifications as well.[8] They were now able to have children. They and their posterity also became subject to injury, disease, and death. And a loving Creator blessed them with healing power by which the life and function of precious physical bodies could be preserved. For example, bones, if broken, could become solid again. Lacerations of the flesh could heal themselves. And miraculously, leaks in the circulation could be sealed off by components activated from the very blood being lost.[9]

Think of the wonder of that power to heal! If you could create anything that could repair itself, you would have created life in perpetuity. For example, if you could create a chair that could fix its own broken leg, there would be no limit to the life of that chair. Many of you walk on legs that were once broken and do so because of your remarkable gift of healing.

Even though our Creator endowed us with this incredible power, He consigned a counterbalancing gift to our bodies. It is the blessing of *aging,* with visible reminders that we are mortal beings destined one day to leave this "frail existence."[10] Our bodies change every day. As we grow older, our broad chests and narrow waists have a tendency to trade places. We get wrinkles, lose color in our hair—even the hair itself—to remind us that we are mortal children of God, with a "manufacturer's guarantee" that we shall not be stranded upon the earth forever. Were it not for the Fall, our physicians, beauticians, and morticians would all be unemployed.

Adam and Eve—as mortal beings—were instructed to "worship the Lord their God, and . . . offer the firstlings of their flocks, for an offering unto the Lord."[11] They were further instructed that "the life of the flesh is in the blood: . . . for it is the blood that maketh an atonement for the soul."[12] Probation, procreation, and aging were all components of—and physical death was essential to—God's "great plan of happiness."[13]

But mortal life, glorious as it is, was never the *ultimate* objective of God's plan. Life and death here on planet Earth were merely *means* to an end—not the *end* for which we were sent.

## ATONEMENT

That brings us to the Atonement. Paul said, "As in Adam all die, even so in Christ shall all be made alive."[14] The Atonement of Jesus Christ became the *immortal creation*. He volunteered to answer the ends of a law previously transgressed.[15] And by the shedding of His blood, His[16] and our physical bodies could become perfected. They could again function without blood, just as Adam's and Eve's did in their *paradisiacal* form. Paul taught that "flesh and blood cannot inherit the kingdom of God; . . . this mortal must put on immortality."[17]

## MEANING OF ATONEMENT

With this background in mind, let us now ponder the deep meaning of the word *atonement*. In the English language, the components are *at-one-ment,* suggesting that a person is at one with another. Other languages[18] employ words that connote either *expiation* or *reconciliation. Expiation* means "to atone for." *Reconciliation* comes from Latin roots *re,* meaning "again"; *con,* meaning

165

"with"; and *sella,* meaning "seat." *Reconciliation,* therefore, liter-ally means "to sit again with."

Rich meaning is found in study of the word *atonement* in the Semitic languages of Old Testament times. In Hebrew, the basic word for atonement is *kaphar,* a verb that means "to cover" or "to forgive."[19] Closely related is the Aramaic and Arabic word *kafat,* meaning "a close embrace"—no doubt related to the Egyptian ritual embrace. References to that embrace are evident in the Book of Mormon. One states that "the Lord hath redeemed my soul . . . ; I have beheld his glory, and I am encircled about eter-nally in the arms of his love."[20] Another proffers the glorious hope of our being "clasped in the arms of Jesus."[21]

I weep for joy when I contemplate the significance of it all. To be redeemed is to be atoned—received in the close embrace of God, with an expression not only of His forgiveness, but of our oneness of heart and mind. What a privilege! And what a comfort to those of us with loved ones who have already passed from our family circle through the gateway we call death!

Scriptures teach us more about the word *atonement.* The Old Testament has many references to *atonement,* which called for ani-mal sacrifice. Not any animal would do. Special considerations included:

• the selection of a firstling of the flock, without blemish,[22]
• the sacrifice of the animal's life by the shedding of its blood,[23]
• death of the animal without breaking a bone,[24] and
• one animal could be sacrificed as a vicarious act for another.[25]

The Atonement of Christ fulfilled these prototypes of the Old Testament. He was the firstborn Lamb of God, without blemish. His sacrifice occurred by the shedding of blood. No bones of His body were broken—noteworthy in that both malefactors crucified with the Lord had their legs broken.[26] And His was a vicarious sacrifice for others.

While the words *atone* or *atonement,* in any of their forms, appear only once in the King James translation of the New Testament,[27] they appear thirty-five times in the Book of Mormon.[28] As another testament of Jesus Christ, it sheds precious light on His Atonement, as do the Doctrine and Covenants and the Pearl of Great Price. Latter-day revelation has added much to our biblical base of understanding.

## INFINITE ATONEMENT

In preparatory times of the Old Testament, the practice of atonement was finite—meaning it had an end. It was a symbolic forecast of the definitive atonement of Jesus the Christ. His Atonement is infinite—without an end.[29] It was also infinite in that all humankind would be saved from never-ending death. It was infinite in terms of His immense suffering. It was infinite in time, putting an end to the preceding prototype of animal sacrifice. It was infinite in scope—it was to be done once for all.[30] And the mercy of the Atonement extends not only to an infinite number of people, but also to an infinite number of worlds created by Him.[31] It was infinite beyond any human scale of measurement or mortal comprehension.

Jesus was the only one who could offer such an infinite atonement, since He was born of a mortal mother and an immortal Father. Because of that unique birthright, Jesus was an infinite Being.

## THE ORDEAL OF THE ATONEMENT

The ordeal of the Atonement centered about the city of Jerusalem. There the greatest single act of love of all recorded history took place.[32] Leaving the upper room, Jesus and His friends crossed the deep ravine east of the city and came to a garden of olive trees on the lower slopes of the Mount of Olives. There in the garden bearing the Hebrew name of Gethsemane—meaning "oil-press"—olives had been beaten and pressed to provide oil and food. There at Gethsemane, the Lord "suffered the pain of all men, that all . . . might repent and come unto him."[33] He took upon Himself the weight of the sins of all mankind, bearing its massive load that caused Him to bleed from every pore.[34]

Later, He was beaten and scourged. A crown of sharp thorns was thrust upon His head as an additional form of torture.[35] He was mocked and jeered. He suffered every indignity at the hands of His own people. "I came unto my own," He said, "and my own received me not."[36] Instead of their warm embrace, He received their cruel rejection. Then He was required to carry His own cross to the hill of Calvary, where He was nailed to that cross and made to suffer excruciating pain.

Later He said, "I thirst."[37] To a doctor of medicine, this is a very meaningful expression. Doctors know that when a patient goes into shock because of blood loss, invariably that patient—if still conscious—with parched and shriveled lips—cries for water.

Even though the Father and the Son knew well in advance what was to be experienced, the actuality of it brought indescribable agony. "And [Jesus] said, Abba, Father, all things are possible unto thee; take away this cup from me: nevertheless not what I will, but what thou wilt."[38] Jesus then complied with the will of His Father.[39] Three days later—precisely as prophesied—He rose from the grave. He became the firstfruits of the Resurrection. He had accomplished the Atonement, which could give immortality and eternal life to all obedient human beings.

All that the Fall allowed to go awry, the Atonement allowed to go aright.

The Savior's gift of *immortality* comes to all who have ever lived. But His gift of *eternal life* requires repentance and obedience to specific ordinances and covenants. Essential ordinances of the gospel symbolize the Atonement. Baptism by immersion is symbolic of the death, burial, and resurrection of the Redeemer. Partaking of the sacrament renews baptismal covenants and also renews our memory of the Savior's broken flesh and of the blood He shed for us. Ordinances of the temple symbolize our reconciliation with the Lord and seal families together forever. Obedience to the sacred covenants made in temples qualifies us for eternal life—the greatest gift of God to man[40]—the "object and end of our existence."[41]

## THE ATONEMENT ENABLED THE PURPOSE OF THE CREATION TO BE ACCOMPLISHED

The Creation required the Fall. The Fall required the Atonement. The Atonement enabled the purpose of the Creation to be accomplished. Eternal life, made possible by the Atonement, is the supreme purpose of the Creation. To phrase that statement in its negative form, if families were not sealed in holy temples, the whole earth would be utterly wasted.[42]

The purposes of the Creation, the Fall, and the Atonement all converge on the sacred work done in temples of The Church of Jesus Christ of Latter-day Saints. The earth was created and the Church was restored to make possible the sealing of wife to husband, children to parents, families to progenitors, worlds without end.

This is the great latter-day work of which we are a part. That is why we have missionaries; that is why we have temples—to bring the fullest blessings of the Atonement to faithful children of God. That is why we respond to our own calls from the Lord. When we comprehend His voluntary Atonement, any sense of sacrifice on our part becomes completely overshadowed by a profound sense of gratitude for the privilege of serving Him.

As one of "the special witnesses of the name of Christ in all the world,"[43] I testify that He is the Son of the living God. Jesus is the Christ—our atoning Savior and Redeemer. This is His Church, restored to bless God's children and to prepare the world for the Second Coming of the Lord.

NOTES

1. Jacob 4:12.

2. The relationships of these components are found linked together in several scriptures, such as Alma 18:34–39; Mormon 9:12; D&C 20:17–24.

3. They were created as *amortal* beings—"without mortality"—not presently subject to death.

4. See Alma 12:21–23.

5. 2 Nephi 2:23.

6. See Genesis 1:28; Moses 2:28.

7. 2 Nephi 2:25.

8. We should remember that God forgave Adam and Eve their transgression (see Moses 6:53).

9. Such as platelets and thrombin.

10. Eliza R. Snow, "O My Father," *Hymns*, no. 292.

11. Moses 5:5.

12. Leviticus 17:11.

13. See Alma 42:8.

14. 1 Corinthians 15:22; see also Mosiah 16:7–8.

15. See 2 Nephi 2:7; see also "Behold the Great Redeemer Die," *Hymns*, no. 191.

16. See Luke 13:32.

17. 1 Corinthians 15:50–53.

18. Such as Spanish, Portuguese, French, Italian, and German.

19. We might even surmise that if an individual qualifies for the blessings of the Atonement (through obedience to the principles and ordinances of the gospel), Jesus will "cover" our past transgressions against the Father.

20. 2 Nephi 1:15.

21. Mormon 5:11; additional examples are in Alma 5:33; 34:16.

22. See Leviticus 5:18; 27:26.

23. See Leviticus 9:18.

24. See Exodus 12:46; Numbers 9:12.

25. See Leviticus 16:10.

26. See John 19:31–33.

27. See Romans 5:11.

28. *Atonement* = 24; plus *atone, atoning,* or *atoned* = 8; plus *atoneth* = 3—a total of 35 times.

29. See 2 Nephi 9:7; 25:16; Alma 34:10, 12, 14.

30. See Hebrews 10:10.

31. See D&C 76:24; Moses 1:33.

32. See John 3:16.

33. D&C 18:11.

34. See Luke 22:44; D&C 19:18.

35. See Matthew 27:29; Mark 15:17; John 19:2, 5.

36. 3 Nephi 9:16; see also D&C 6:21; 10:57; 11:29; 39:3; 45:8; 133:66.

37. John 19:28.

38. Mark 14:36. The word *Abba* is significant. *Ab* means "father"; *Abba* is an endearing and tender form of that term. The nearest English equivalent might be *Daddy.*

39. Centuries later, the Lord shared innermost recollections of this experience with the Prophet Joseph Smith, the record of which we read in D&C 19.

40. See D&C 14:7.

41. Bruce R. McConkie, *The Promised Messiah* (Salt Lake City: Deseret Book Co., 1978), 568.

42. See D&C 2:3; 138:48.

43. D&C 107:23.

# WHY THIS HOLY LAND?

---

Have you ever wondered why the Lord chose to accomplish His mortal ministry in the exact location that He did? He created the earth. In His divine role, He could have selected any portion of this bounteous planet to accomplish His mission. He could have selected the beautiful islands of the sea with their lush vegetation and breathtaking beauty. He could have chosen the scenery of Switzerland or Scandinavia, or He could have preferred to walk upon the acres of Africa or Australia.

Instead, He selected the land with places stark and arid, but made holy by His presence there. He did so for many reasons, including His desire to teach with geographical visual aids, and to fulfill scripture.

### BIRTH IN BETHLEHEM

This is a land where nomads dwell, living in tents and wandering as freely as the sheep and goats that they tend. He chose to be born in Bethlehem, adjoining Jerusalem. This He did to teach symbolically and to fulfill scriptural prophecy. Years before this event the prophet Micah foretold:

"But thou, Bethlehem . . . though thou be little among the

thousands of Judah, yet out of thee shall he come forth unto me that is to be ruler in Israel; whose goings forth have been from of old, from everlasting."[1]

The Book of Mormon also records that the Lord's birthplace was foredetermined, as prophesied by Alma eighty-three years before the Savior was born:

"And behold, he shall be born of Mary, at Jerusalem which is the land of our forefathers, she being a virgin, a precious and chosen vessel, who shall be overshadowed and conceive by the power of the Holy Ghost, and bring forth a son, yea, even the Son of God."[2]

Yes, after millennia of preparation, the long awaited event occurred. Christ was born among men. No wonder angelic choirs sang as they knew that extended centuries of death and darkness were to be relieved by the Atonement, which was finally to come through this Babe of Bethlehem.

Why Bethlehem? Is there symbolic significance in the meaning of the name *Bethlehem,* which in Hebrew means "house of bread"? The Great Provider declared Himself to be the "bread of life."[3] How appropriate it was that He, the "bread of life," was to come from the "house of bread."

But why among the animals? He, whom John declared to be the "Lamb of God,"[4] was born during the season of Passover amongst the animals, as were other lambs being prepared for Paschal sacrifice.

At the birth of Him who is called the "good shepherd,"[5] shepherds were the first to receive the announcement of His holy birth.[6]

At the birth of Him who once identified Himself as the "bright and morning star,"[7] a new star appeared in the heavens.[8] Shining brightly over Bethlehem, that star had been placed in orbit far in advance of the foretold event in order that its light could coincide in time and place with His blessed birth.

At the arrival of Him who was called "the light of the world,"[9] darkness was banished as a sign of His holy birth.[10] He was born the Son of God and the son of a virgin mother, as foretold by Isaiah[11] and other prophets.[12]

## EXODUS TO EGYPT

The place of His birth was to be in close proximity to Egypt in order to fulfill other scriptural prophecies. Shortly after His birth, Jesus was taken to Egypt, comparable to travels of earlier Israelites. The sojourn of the Holy Child in Egypt fulfilled the prophecy recorded in Hosea 11:1: "I . . . called my son out of Egypt." That this scripture truly pertained to the Savior was affirmed by Matthew:

"[Joseph] took the young child and his mother by night, and departed into Egypt: . . . that it might be fulfilled which was spoken of the Lord by the prophet, saying, Out of Egypt have I called my son."[13]

## CHILDHOOD IN NAZARETH

But He didn't stay in the spiritual darkness of Egypt very long. As a child, the Savior was brought to the village of Nazareth. Why Nazareth? Again, to fulfill prophecy. Jeremiah foretold:

"Behold, the days come, saith the Lord, that I will raise unto David a righteous Branch, and a King shall reign and prosper."[14]

I am intrigued with the symbolic significance of the fact that some scholars suggest that the word *Nazareth* is derived from the Hebrew word *neser,* which means "branch." Jesus, the divine Branch, was to be reared in the place with the name meaning "branch." Jeremiah further prophesied that the Lord would "cause the Branch of righteousness to grow up unto David; and he shall execute judgment and righteousness in the land."[15]

We read in the Book of Mormon of another interesting connection between "branch" and "Nazareth." Do you remember the reply after Nephi had asked the Lord the meaning of the tree of life? The Lord then revealed to him a glimpse of the city of Nazareth, where Nephi beheld in vision "a virgin, most beautiful and fair." She was destined to become the mother of the Son of God.[16] Isn't it interesting that the little town of Nazareth, which name signifies "branch," was shown to Nephi in vision after his inquiry about the tree of life?

From Matthew 2:23 we learn that Jesus "came and dwelt in a city called Nazareth: that it might be fulfilled which was spoken by the prophets, He shall be called a Nazarene."

## WATER

Much of the Holy Land is desert with very little water. Because water was scarce and precious, it became the object of special lessons taught by the Lord.

The River Jordan was the site Jesus chose for His baptism by John to "fulfill all righteousness."[17] Is it significant that this sacred ordinance was performed in virtually the lowest body of fresh water on the planet? Could He have selected a better place to symbolize the humble depths to which He went and from which He rose? By example, He taught us that He literally descended beneath all things to rise above all things. Surely, being baptized after the manner of His baptism signifies that through our obedience and effort we, too, can come from the depths to ascend to lofty heights of our own destiny.

To us, the River Jordan is a sacred stream. The Jordan marked the termination of the wandering of the children of

Israel. They had journeyed there from the banks of the Nile. Joshua had led some 600,000 Israelite warriors and their families across that roiling river during flood season, when the waters were suddenly stopped and heaped up to allow the faithful Israelites, carrying the ark of the covenant, to cross an empty riverbed.[18]

We don't know the precise location where this crossing occurred or the exact spot where Jesus was baptized. Both the Bible and the Book of Mormon indicate that the baptism took place in the vicinity of Bethabara.[19] Bethabara in Hebrew means "house of the crossing."

Time and again, we quote the statement of Jesus to Nicodemus. To him the Savior declared, "Except a man be born of water and of the Spirit, he cannot enter into the kingdom of God."[20] Could it be that Christ chose this location for His baptism in the River Jordan as a silent commemoration of the crossing of those faithful Israelites under Joshua's direction so many years before, as well as a symbol that baptism is a spiritual crossing into the kingdom of God?

Amidst wilderness and desert isolation such as this, the Savior was able to teach important lessons that only those who knew what it was to be thirsty could fully appreciate. To the woman of Samaria at the well He said:

"Whosoever drinketh of this water shall thirst again:

"But whosoever drinketh of the water that I shall give him shall never thirst; but the water that I shall give him shall be in him a well of water springing up into everlasting life."[21]

The Savior brought His disciples a great distance to teach at a place called Caesarea Philippi, where He asked them this crucial question: "Whom do men say that I the Son of man am?"

Simon Peter gave his inspired answer: "Thou art the Christ, the Son of the living God.

176

"And Jesus answered, and said unto him, Blessed art thou, Simon Bar-jona: for flesh and blood hath not revealed it unto thee, but my Father which is in heaven. . . . Upon this rock I will build my church; and the gates of hell shall not prevail against it."[22]

The modern-day scene in Caesarea Philippi is unique. There is a mountain at the base of which is a mighty rock from which water seems to be flowing. These cascades comprise one of the three major headwaters of the River Jordan, literally the liquid lifeline of this country. As Jesus was preparing to conclude His mortal ministry, here He trained future leaders of His Church. Could it be that the Savior brought His disciples to this spot to teach the lesson that this majestic mountain symbolized the rock of Christ from whom revelation would flow?—revelation to bring light and life to them, just as that flowing water of the River Jordan nourishes Israel.

## MOUNTAINS

Other mountains in the land were also made holy by Jesus. He employed them as spiritual and visual aids to teach His followers.

Nearly a week after the Lord was with His disciples at Caesarea Philippi, Jesus took "Peter, James, and John his brother, and bringeth them up into an high mountain apart,

"And was transfigured before them: and . . . there appeared unto them Moses and [Elijah]."[23]

Scholars do not know for sure whether Mount Hermon or Mount Tabor was the actual site of the Transfiguration. What is more important is that Moses and Elijah there conferred keys of the priesthood, under the direction of the Lord, on Peter, James, and John.

Remarkable is the fact that Moses and Elijah were those who

177

conferred those same special keys upon Joseph Smith and Oliver Cowdery in the Kirtland Temple, 3 April 1836, just one week after the dedication of that temple.[24]

For centuries faithful Jews have anticipated the return of Elijah at the Passover. Isn't it interesting that the date of 3 April 1836 was one of the few times when Easter Sunday coincided with the beginning of Passover? Elijah did return as had been hoped, at the Passover, on Easter, to restore keys of the sealing power that were uniquely assigned to him to convey.

Those same keys are used today to effect eternal linkage in the holy temples of the Lord. We know that the Lord will honor these ordinances, performed by His duly authorized agents, as He declared, "Whatsoever ye shall bind on earth shall be bound in heaven: and whatsoever ye shall loose on earth shall be loosed in heaven."[25] Each such eternal ordinance is performed in a holy temple, appropriately known as a "mountain of the Lord's house."[26]

Mountains were often used anciently for the same purposes temples are used today. Moses, for example, was brought to Mount Sinai to be instructed there by the Lord.

Mountains are not easy to climb. Then, as now, the Lord called His disciples to climb mountains to emphasize the efficacy of effort and obedience. He will ask the same of you, figuratively and possibly literally, also.

Christ again used a mountain to emphasize effort in His Sermon on the Mount. While speaking near the northern shore of the Sea of Galilee, He commanded His disciples to be perfect even as their Father in Heaven. They were taught the principles of prayer. They were commanded to seek first the kingdom of God and His righteousness. The Lord promised salvation to those who followed His example in doing the will of His Father.[27]

There is another important mountain known in today's

Israel, as in yesteryear, as Mount Moriah. Now ornamented by objects and mosques of man, it still suggests sacred recollection of the obedience and faith of Abraham and Isaac. Their long three-day journey from Beersheba to Mount Moriah was taken at the request of God. *Moriah* in the Hebrew language means "seen or chosen by Jehovah."

The first sacred temple of Jerusalem was constructed on Mount Moriah. At that site, Jesus attended the remodeled second temple. Initially He called it "my Father's house."[28] There He accomplished the first cleansing of the temple by driving out the money-changers.

At the time of the second cleansing, He called it "my house." And He said unto them, "It is written, My house shall be called the house of prayer; but ye have made it a den of thieves."[29]

Finally and sadly, He called it "your house" when He said in desperation, "Behold, your house is left unto you desolate,"[30] and predicted the destruction of Jerusalem and the temple, of which one stone would not be left upon the other. How could these important messages regarding the temple have been delivered in any other land? For His own mortal ministry He chose the land with the temple.

## LOCAL KNOWLEDGE AND SITES

Underground tombs were commonly used for interment of the dead. Jesus was elsewhere when His dear friend Lazarus died. But the Lord knew very well what had transpired. The scriptural account relates that not until Lazarus had been dead *four days* did Jesus appear on the scene. At that late date Martha, sister of Lazarus, exclaimed, "By this time he stinketh."[31]

Jesus then "cried with a loud voice, Lazarus, come forth.

"And he that was dead came forth, bound hand and foot with

179

graveclothes: and his face was bound about with a napkin. Jesus saith unto them, Loose him, and let him go.

"Then many . . . believed on [the Lord]."[32]

There is great significance to the four-day interval between the death of Lazarus and his being called forth alive from the tomb. A portion of that significance was that, according to some Jewish traditions, it took four days before the Spirit finally and irrevocably departed from the body of the deceased person, so that decomposition could then proceed. The Master, in order to demonstrate His total power over death and His control over life, knowingly waited until that four-day interval had elapsed. Then He raised Lazarus from the dead!

Toward the end of His mortal ministry, the Messiah entered the old city of Jerusalem, riding upon a donkey. This, too, was in fulfillment of scriptural prophecy.

"Thy King cometh unto thee: he is just, and having salvation; lowly, and riding upon an ass, and upon a colt the foal of an ass."[33]

That prophecy of Zechariah could hardly have been fulfilled if the Savior had ministered in any other locale.

Olive trees are special in the Holy Land. The olive branch is universally regarded as a symbol of peace. This tree provides food, light, heat, lumber, ointments, and medicine. It is now, as it was then, crucial to life in Israel. It is not a deciduous tree, but everbearing—always green. Even if the tree is chopped down, life will spring from its roots, suggesting everlasting life. Jewish tradition often refers to the olive tree as the tree of life. To me it seems to prefigure the Resurrection.

### SITES AND SYMBOLS OF THE ATONEMENT

Jesus came to the base of the Mount of Olives to effect the first component of the Atonement. This He did at the Garden of Gethsemane. The word *Gethsemane* comes from two Hebrew roots: *gath,* meaning "press," and *shemen,* meaning "oil," especially that of the olive.

There olives had been pressed under the weight of great stone wheels to squeeze precious oil from the olives. So the Christ in the Garden of Gethsemane was literally pressed under the weight of the sins of the world. He sweated great drops of blood—his life's "oil"—which issued from every pore.[34]

Jesus was accorded titles of unique significance. One was the *Messiah,* which in Hebrew means "anointed." The other was the *Christ,* which in the Greek language means "anointed" as well. In our day, as it was in His day, the ordinance of administration to the sick includes anointing with the consecrated oil of the olive. So the next time you witness consecrated oil being anointed on the head of one to be blessed, and these sacred words are said, "I anoint you with this consecrated oil," remember what that original consecration cost. Remember what it meant to all who had ever lived and who ever would yet live. Remember the redemptive power of healing, soothing, and ministering to those in need. Remember, just as the body of the olive, which was pressed for the oil that gave light, so the Savior was pressed. From every pore oozed the lifeblood of our Redeemer. Throughout the joyous days of your life's mission, when your cup of gladness runs over, remember His cup of bitterness which made it possible. And when sore trials come upon you, remember Gethsemane.

The second phase of His atonement was effected on the cross. Hours before that was accomplished, Barabbas was released and, in his stead, Jesus the Christ was consigned to the cross. Ironic it is that *Barabbas* in local language literally means "son of the father." While he was released, the true Son of the Eternal Father was condemned to death.[35]

Pilate delivered the Lamb of God to be crucified at the same time Paschal lambs nearby were being prepared for sacrifice.[36]

The Crucifixion took place at a hill called Golgotha (Greek) or Calvary (Latin) meaning "the skull." The skull symbolized death. At a place such as this, the atoning sacrifice was completed. On the cross, the Savior of the world was lifted up over death in the greatest of all possible significance—the realization and reality of the Lord's power over death.

God the Father offered His son Jesus at Golgotha (or Calvary), a northern outcropping of Mount Moriah, where Abraham had nearly sacrificed Isaac some two thousand years previously. Foreseen long before, there the Savior's atoning sacrifice was completed.

But of course that was not the end. It was but a new beginning. The reality of the Resurrection was the most glorious event of all. The Apostle Paul wrote that after three days in the tomb Jesus had "risen from the dead, and become the firstfruits of them that slept. . . .

"For as in Adam all die, even so in Christ shall all be made alive."[37]

As a resurrected personage, the Lord charged His disciples with this important responsibility: "Go ye into all the world, and preach the gospel to every creature."[38]

"Go ye therefore, and teach all nations, baptizing them in the name of the Father, and of the Son, and of the Holy Ghost:

"Teaching them to observe all things whatsoever I have commanded you: and, lo, I am with you alway, even unto the end of the world."[39]

### FUTURE

This charge still applies to each of us. All true disciples of the Lord bear that sacred responsibility.

But the Savior's ministry was not limited to the Holy Land.

He spoke of "other sheep I have, which are not of this fold: . . . they shall hear my voice."[40]

Love for those other sheep brought the resurrected Lord to them here on the American hemisphere.[41] He taught the gospel to them. Here He established His church. He charged them with the responsibility of keeping records of His ministry among them.

This precious record we received from them as the Book of Mormon is the great clarifying scripture. It is the great missionary scripture. It is another testament of Jesus Christ. Its four major writers—Nephi, Jacob, Mormon, and Moroni—were all eyewitnesses of the Son of God. No wonder this sacred text has become our great and valuable friend as we teach and testify of the Lord.

We testify that God our Father, and His Son, Jesus Christ, appeared to the Prophet Joseph Smith in upstate New York in 1820. There and then the promised restitution of all things was begun. The great latter-day work of which we are a part was established, on schedule, to bless a waiting and weeping world.

But eventually the Lord will return to the land that He made holy by His mission there in mortality. In triumph, He will come again to Jerusalem. In flaming royal robes of red to symbolize His blood, which oozed from every pore, He shall return to the Holy City. There and elsewhere, "the glory of the Lord shall be revealed, and all flesh shall see it together."[42] His "name shall be called Wonderful, Counsellor, The mighty God, The everlasting Father, The Prince of Peace."[43]

The significance of the Holy Land as headquarters of the Lord's ministry is not all in the past. Other prophecies are yet to be fulfilled in the future. Ultimately, at the onset of His millennial reign, Christ shall come again. The Mount of Olives to which He will return "shall cleave in twain."[44] When He appears, He will utter these words:

"I was wounded in the house of my friends. I am he who was lifted up. I am Jesus that was crucified. I am the Son of God."[45]

Our sacred charge is to prepare the world for that glorious second coming of the Lord.

Another temple will yet be built in Jerusalem. Water will issue from under the temple. Waters of the Dead Sea will be healed. All this and more will occur prior to the promised second coming of our King. From that temple He shall reign forever as Lord of Lords.

Nothing in the Savior's life was without supernal significance or eternal consequence. He used locations available during His mortal ministry to fulfill prophecy and to teach in His "more excellent way."[46]

As I contemplate our call to stand as witnesses of Christ "at all times and in all things, and in all places,"[47] I think of a special scripture. After the priesthood had been given to the Lord's Apostles, as His Father had given it to Him before, Jesus said, "As my Father hath sent me, even so send I you."[48] Praying to His Father, He concluded, "And the glory [which is the priesthood] which thou gavest me I have given them; that they may be one, even as we are one."[49]

So we are one, my beloved brothers and sisters, united in this cause and in the glory of Him who has sent us forth on His errand. May we sense and appreciate the symbolic significance of His mortal ministry in this Holy Land. May we understand His ministry to other sheep that He loved. May we realize our role in the restoration He has required, to prepare the world for His second coming. May we comprehend the eternal consequences of the endless life of our Lord, whose servants we are. May we have power and strength to motivate ourselves to do His will in the mountainous responsibilities that are before us.

NOTES

    1. Micah 5:2.

    2. Alma 7:10.

    3. See John 6:48.

    4. John 1:29.

    5. John 10:14.

    6. See Luke 2:8–16.

    7. Revelation 22:16.

    8. See Matthew 2:2, 3 Nephi 1:21.

    9. John 8:12.

10. See 3 Nephi 1:15, 19.

11. See Isaiah 7:14.

12. See 1 Nephi 11:13–21; Alma 7:9–10.

13. Matthew 2:14–15.

14. Jeremiah 23:5.

15. Jeremiah 33:15.

16. See 1 Nephi 11:8–18.

17. Matthew 3:15; see also 2 Nephi 31:5–6.

18. See Joshua 3.

19. See John 1:28, 1 Nephi 10:9; JST, John 1:34.

20. John 3:5.

21. John 4:13–14.

22. Matthew 16:13, 16–18.

23. Matthew 17:1–3.

24. See D&C 110:11–16.

25. Matthew 18:18.

26. Isaiah 2:2, see also 2 Nephi 12:2.

27. See Matthew 5–7.

28. John 2:16.

29. Matthew 21:13.

30. Luke 13:35.

31. John 11:39.

32. John 11:43–45.

33. Zechariah 9:9.

34. See Luke 22:44; D&C 19:18.

35. See Matthew 27:17–26.

36. See John 19:13–14.

37. 1 Corinthians 15:20, 22.

38. Mark 16:15.

39. Matthew 28:19–20.

40. John 10:16.

41. See 3 Nephi 15:21.

42. Isaiah 40:5.

43. Isaiah 9:6; see also 2 Nephi 19:6.

44. D&C 45:48.

45. D&C 45:52.

46. 1 Corinthians 12:31; see also Ether 12:11.

47. Mosiah 18:9.

48. John 20:21; see also 17:18.

49. John 17:22.

# CHILDREN OF THE COVENANT

In introducing the topic "children of the covenant,"[1] I will reflect upon events I experienced as a colleague of President Howard W. Hunter, as a father, and as a doctor of medicine.

Several weeks in early 1995 were extremely challenging for Sister Nelson and me. Not only did we bid farewell to our beloved President Hunter, but thirty-three days earlier, we suffered the demise of our precious daughter, Emily. A mother of five young children, Emily had just celebrated her thirty-seventh birthday when called to the other side.

President Hunter influenced Emily's life in a real way. She welcomed his invitation for all adult members of the Church to hold a temple recommend. She and her husband, Bradley Wittwer, regarded their regular time in the temple as a sacred privilege. They viewed "the temple of the Lord as the great symbol of their membership and the supernal setting for their most sacred covenants." She strived to emulate the "example of the Lord Jesus Christ."[2]

Even though illness brought intense suffering to President Hunter and Emily, an angry word never fell from their lips. Instead, they chose to endure with loving faith. When well-meaning friends and family expressed concern for Emily, she

187

cheerfully replied, "Don't worry, I'll be OK!" Even when she concluded a telephone call, she did not close with the customary "good-bye." She would say, "I love you!"

When President Boyd K. Packer and I last visited President Hunter, he beckoned for Sister Hunter, reached for her hand, and said with a smile, "I feel better when you are near me."

My tears of sorrow have flowed along with wishes that I could have done more for our daughter and for our President. If I had the power of resurrection, I would have been tempted to bring them back. Though one of the ordained Apostles, each of whom is entrusted with all the keys of the kingdom of God, I do not hold keys of the Resurrection. Jesus Christ holds those keys and will use them for Emily, for President Hunter, and for all people in the Lord's own time.[3]

Emily and President Hunter had no fear of death. They had made and honored sacred covenants with the Lord, and they knew that his covenants to them will be kept with equal fidelity.[4] They lived nobly as "children of the covenant."

Years ago as a young medical student, I saw many patients afflicted with diseases that are now preventable. Today it is possible to immunize individuals against conditions that once were disabling—even deadly. One medical method by which acquired immunity is conferred is inoculation. The term *inoculate* is fascinating. It comes from two Latin roots: *in,* meaning "within"; and *oculus,* meaning "an eye." The verb to *inoculate,* therefore, literally means "to put an eye within"—to monitor against harm.

An affliction like polio can cripple or destroy the body. An affliction like sin can cripple or destroy the spirit. The ravages of polio can now be prevented by immunization, but the ravages of sin require other means of prevention. Doctors cannot immunize against iniquity. Spiritual protection comes only from the Lord[5]—and in His own way. Jesus chooses not to inoculate, but to indoctrinate. His method employs no vaccine; it utilizes the teaching of divine doctrine—a governing "eye within"—to protect the eternal spirits of His children.

## IDENTIFICATION AND INDOCTRINATION

In so teaching, Jesus often established His own identity,[6] then the identity of His followers. I quote His words to the people of ancient America. He said, "*I* am Jesus Christ, the Son of God."[7]

"All the prophets from Samuel and those that follow after . . . have testified of *me*.

"And behold, *ye* are the children of the prophets; and *ye* are of the house of Israel; and *ye* are of the covenant which the Father made with your fathers, saying unto Abraham: And in thy seed shall all the kindreds of the earth be blessed.

"The Father having raised *me* up unto you first, and sent *me* to bless *you* in turning away every one of you from his iniquities; and this because *ye* are the children of the covenant."[8]

A giant step toward spiritual immunity is taken when we understand the expression "children of the covenant." To what covenant did the Savior refer? "The covenant which he made with Abraham."[9] The Lord added, "I will remember the covenant which I have made with my people; and I have covenanted with them that I would gather them together *in mine own due time*."[10]

## THE ABRAHAMIC COVENANT

The covenant that the Lord first made to Abraham[11] and reaffirmed to Isaac[12] and Jacob[13] is of transcendent significance. It contained several promises:

• Abraham's posterity would be numerous, entitled to eternal increase and to bear the priesthood;

• He would become a father of many nations;

189

• Christ and kings would come through Abraham's lineage;

• Certain lands would be inherited;

• All nations of the earth would be blessed by his seed;

• That covenant would be everlasting—even through "a thousand generations."[14]

Some of these promises have been accomplished; others have yet to be. I quote from a prophecy given nearly 600 years B.C.: "Our father hath not spoken of our seed alone, but also of all the house of Israel, pointing to the covenant which should be *fulfilled in the latter days;* which covenant the Lord made to our father Abraham."[15]

Precisely as promised, the Master appeared in these latter days to renew the Abrahamic covenant. To the Prophet Joseph Smith the Lord declared: "Abraham received promises concerning his seed, and of the fruit of his loins—from whose loins ye are, . . . my servant Joseph. . . . This promise is yours also, because ye are of Abraham."[16]

We are also children of the covenant. We have received, as did they of old, the holy priesthood and the everlasting gospel. Abraham, Isaac, and Jacob are our ancestors. We are of Israel. We have the right to receive the gospel, blessings of the priesthood, and eternal life. Nations of the earth will be blessed by our efforts and by the labors of our posterity. The literal seed of Abraham and those who are gathered into his family by adoption receive these promised blessings—predicated upon acceptance of the Lord and obedience to His commandments.

Elijah the prophet came to plant a knowledge of these promises made to the fathers.[17] Later, the Book of Mormon came forth as a sign that the Lord had commenced to gather children of the covenant.[18] This book, written for our day, states: "Then ye may know that the covenant which the Father hath made with the children of Israel . . . is already beginning to be fulfilled. . . .

190

"For behold, the Lord will remember his covenant which he hath made unto his people of the house of Israel."[19]

## THE NEW AND EVERLASTING COVENANT

Indeed, the Lord has not forgotten us. And to ensure that we do not forget him, children of the covenant receive His doctrine and claim it by covenant. Brigham Young said: "All Latter-day Saints enter the new and everlasting covenant when they enter this Church. . . . They enter the new and everlasting covenant to sustain the Kingdom of God and no other kingdom."[20]

At baptism, we covenant to serve the Lord and keep His commandments. When we partake of the sacrament, we renew those covenants. We may receive covenants of the priesthood[21] and the crowning blessings of the endowment, the doctrine, and the covenants unique to the holy temple.

The new and everlasting covenant of the gospel allows us to qualify for marriage in the temple and be blessed to "come forth in the first resurrection" and "inherit thrones, kingdoms, principalities, and powers, dominions, . . . to [our] exaltation and glory in all things."[22]

Children born to parents thus married are natural heirs to the blessings of the priesthood. They are born *in the covenant*. Hence, "they require no rite of adoption or sealing to insure their place in the posterity of promise."[23]

Rewards for obedience to the commandments are almost beyond mortal comprehension. Here, children of the covenant become a strain of sin-resistant souls. And hereafter, President Hunter, Emily, other children of the covenant, and "each generation would be linked to the one which went on before . . . [in] the divine family of God."[24] Great comfort comes from the knowledge that our loved ones are secured to us through the covenants.

## UNITY AMONG CHILDREN OF THE COVENANT

Latter-day Saints understand the word of the Lord, who declared, "I say unto you, be one; and if ye are not one ye are not mine."[25]

"This great unity is the hallmark of the true church of Christ," said President Gordon B. Hinckley. "It is felt among our people throughout the world." President Hinckley continued, "We pray for one another that we may go on in unity and strength."[26]

Throughout the world, however, strident voices are engaged in divisive disputation and name-calling. Often demeaning nicknames are added to—or even substituted for—given names. Unfortunately, terms of derision obscure the true identity of children of the covenant.

In contrast, God employs names that unify and sanctify. When we embrace the gospel and are baptized, we are born again and take upon ourselves the sacred name of Jesus Christ.[27] We are adopted as His sons and daughters and are known as brothers and sisters. He is the Father of our new life. We become joint heirs to promises given by the Lord to Abraham, Isaac, Jacob, and their posterity.[28]

Peter used uplifting terms in a prophecy regarding our day. He identified members of the Church as "a chosen generation, a royal priesthood, an holy nation, a *peculiar* people."[29] We recognize the adjectives *chosen, royal,* and *holy* as complimentary. But what about the term *peculiar?*

A modern dictionary defines *peculiar* as "unusual," "eccentric," or "strange."[30] What kind of compliment is that?

But the term *peculiar* as used in the scriptures means something quite different. In the Old Testament, the Hebrew term from which *peculiar* was translated is *segullah,* which means "valued property," or "treasure."[31] In the New Testament, the Greek term from which *peculiar* was translated is *peripoiesis,* which means "possession," or "an obtaining."[32]

With that understanding, we can see that the scriptural term *peculiar* signifies "valued treasure," "made" or "selected by God."[33] Thus, for us to be identified by servants of the Lord as His *peculiar* people is a compliment of the highest order.

When we know who we are and what God expects of us— when His "law [is] written in [our] hearts"[34]—we are spiritually protected. We become better people. When the Nephites were truly righteous, they avoided divisive nicknames and "there was no contention in the land, because of the love of God which did dwell in the hearts of the people."[35]

"There were no . . . Lamanites, nor any manner of -ites; but they were in one, the children of Christ, and heirs to the kingdom of God."[36]

That lesson from history suggests that we also delete from our personal vocabularies names that segregate and hyphens that separate. Paul taught that "there is neither Jew nor Greek, there is neither bond nor free, there is neither male nor female: for ye are all one in Christ Jesus."[37]

He invites us "to come unto him and partake of his goodness; and he denieth none that come unto him, black and white, bond and free, male and female; . . . all are alike unto God."[38]

The Church of Jesus Christ of Latter-day Saints has been restored in these latter days to fulfill ancient promises of the Lord. It is part of the "restitution of all things."[39] Committed children of the covenant remain steadfast, even in the midst of adversity. We shall "be chastened and tried, even as Abraham, who was commanded to offer up his only son."[40] Yet we are strengthened by this promise of the Lord: "Ye are lawful heirs, according to the flesh, and have been hid from the world with Christ in God—

"Therefore your life and the priesthood have remained, and

must needs remain through you and your lineage until the restoration of all things. . . .

"Therefore, blessed are ye if ye continue in my goodness, a light unto the Gentiles, and through this priesthood, a savior unto my people Israel."[41]

With that doctrine implanted deeply within our souls, the sting of death is soothed and spiritual protection is provided. Children of the covenant will be blessed—here and hereafter.

NOTES

1. 3 Nephi 20:26.

2. Howard W. Hunter, quoted in *Ensign,* July 1994, 4–5.

3. See *Discourses of Brigham Young,* sel. John A. Widtsoe (Salt Lake City: Deseret Book Co., 1978), 397–98; Joseph Fielding Smith, *Doctrines of Salvation,* 1:128.

4. See D&C 82:10.

5. Rules of agency and accountability still apply, however. Choice and accountability are divine gifts nearly as precious as life itself. "Even the children of the covenant will be rejected except they make good their title by godly works" (James E. Talmage, *Jesus the Christ* [Salt Lake City: Deseret Book Co., 1976], 540). Children of the covenant are to honor the Sabbath day and keep it holy (see Exodus 31:12–13, 16–17; Ezekiel 20:20) and obey all of God's commandments.

6. For examples, see 3 Nephi 9:15; 11:10; 20:31; Ether 3:14; D&C 6:21; 10:57; 11:28; 14:9; 19:24; 35:2; 36:8; 43:34; 49:28; 51:20; 52:44.

7. 3 Nephi 20:31; emphasis added.

8. 3 Nephi 20:24–26; emphasis added.

9. 3 Nephi 20:27.

10. 3 Nephi 20:29; emphasis added. See also 1 Peter 5:6; 3 Nephi 5:25; Mormon 5:12; D&C 93:19.

11. See Genesis 17:1–10; 22:15–18; Galatians 3:28–29; Abraham 2:9–11.

12. See Genesis 26:1–5, 24.

13. See Genesis 28:1–4, 10–14; 35:9–13; 48:3–4.

14. 1 Chronicles 16:15; see also Genesis 17:1–10, 19; Leviticus 26:42; Acts 3:25; LDS Bible Dictionary, "Abraham, Covenant of," 602.

15. 1 Nephi 15:18; emphasis added. Other prophecies convey similar meaning. Among them are the following:

"Many generations after the Messiah shall be manifested in body unto the children of men, then shall the fulness of the gospel of the Messiah come unto the Gentiles, and from the Gentiles unto the remnant of our seed—

"And at that day shall the remnant of our seed know that they are of the house of Israel, and that they are the covenant people of the Lord; and then shall they know and come to the knowledge of their forefathers, and also to the knowledge of the gospel of their Redeemer, which was ministered unto their fathers by him; wherefore, they shall come to the knowledge of their Redeemer and the very points of his doctrine, that they may know how to come unto him and be saved" (1 Nephi 15:13–14).

"Then will I gather them in from the four quarters of the earth; and then will I fulfil the covenant which the Father hath made unto all the people of the house of Israel" (3 Nephi 16:5).

"And then will I remember my covenant which I have made unto my people, O house of Israel, and I will bring my gospel unto them.

"And I will show unto thee, O house of Israel, that the Gentiles shall not have power over you; but I will remember my covenant unto you, O house of Israel, and ye shall come unto the knowledge of the fulness of my gospel" (3 Nephi 16:11–12).

"Thou shalt preach the fulness of my gospel, which I have sent forth in these last days, the covenant which I have sent forth to recover my people, which are of the house of Israel" (D&C: 39:11).

16. D&C 132:30–31. The Lord also told the Prophet Joseph Smith: "As I said unto Abraham concerning the kindreds of the earth, even so I say unto my servant Joseph: In thee and in thy seed shall the kindred of the earth be blessed" (D&C 124:58).

17. See D&C 2:1–3.

18. See 3 Nephi 29:1–9.

19. 3 Nephi 29:1, 3. As part of that promise, certain lands were to be

inherited. While most descendants of Israel received their inheritance in the Near East, the choice land of the Americas was reserved for Joseph (see Ether 13:8). It was to be the repository of the plates from which the Book of Mormon would be translated. It was also destined to become world headquarters of The Church of Jesus Christ of Latter-day Saints. From there the restored gospel would go forth to bless all nations of the earth—according to the promise. Devout men, women, and children are being gathered in our day, turning to the truths of salvation that they have not heard before.

The Book of Mormon has many prophecies pertaining to the old and new cities of Jerusalem. For example, "Then shall this covenant which the Father hath covenanted with his people be fulfilled; and then shall Jerusalem be inhabited again with my people, and it shall be the land of their inheritance" (3 Nephi 20:46).

"And that it was the place of the New Jerusalem, which should come down out of heaven, and the holy sanctuary of the Lord.

"Behold, Ether saw the days of Christ, and he spake concerning a New Jerusalem upon this land.

"And he spake also concerning the house of Israel, and the Jerusalem from whence Lehi should come—after it should be destroyed it should be built up again, a holy city unto the Lord; wherefore, it could not be a new Jerusalem for it had been in a time of old; but it should be built up again, and become a holy city of the Lord; and it should be built unto the house of Israel—

"And that a New Jerusalem should be built upon this land, unto the remnant of the seed of Joseph, for which things there has been a type" (Ether 13:3–6).

20. *Discourses of Brigham Young,* 160.

21. See D&C 84:39–40.

22. D&C 132:19.

23. James E. Talmage, *The Articles of Faith* (1977), 446.

24. Joseph Fielding Smith, in Conference Report, October 1950, 13–14.

25. D&C 38:27. "Christ and his people will ever be one" (*Hymns,* no. 3).

26. *Ensign,* November 1983, 5.

27. See D&C 20:37.

28. See Galatians 3:29; D&C 86:8–11.

29. 1 Peter 2:9; emphasis added. Moses also employed the term when he said, "Thou art an holy people unto the Lord thy God, and the Lord hath chosen thee to be a *peculiar* people unto himself, above all the nations that are upon the earth" (Deuteronomy 14:2; emphasis added).

30. *The American Heritage Dictionary of the English Language* (New York: Houghton Mifflin Co., 1980), 965.

31. See LDS Bible Dictionary, "Peculiar," 748; "Hebrew and Chaldee Dictionary," *Strong's Exhaustive Concordance of the Bible* (New York: Abingdon Press, 1983), 82, word 5459.

32. Forms of the Greek suffix *poiesis* are seen in words currently in use in the English language. For example, doctors and druggists use a book known as a "pharmaco*poeia,*" which refers to the possession or obtainment of pharmaceutical agents. Students of the English language refer to *onomatopoeia,* a word made to sound like its referent, such as "buzz," "crack," or "twang." The term used for the making of blood in the body is known as hemato*poiesis.*

33. *Peculiar* is used in only seven verses of the Bible. In the Old Testament, it is used five times (see Exodus 19:5; Deuteronomy 14:2; 26:18; Psalm 135:4; Ecclesiastes 2:8). In each instance, it has been translated from the Hebrew term that means "valued treasure."

In the New Testament, *peculiar* is used two times (see Titus 2:14; 1 Peter 2:9). In each instance, it has been translated from a Greek term that signifies "possession," or "those selected by God as His own people."

34. Romans 2:15; see also Jeremiah 31:33; Mosiah 13:11.

35. 4 Nephi 1:15.

36. 4 Nephi 1:17.

37. Galatians 3:28; see also Colossians 3:11. Speaking of correct names, we are reminded of a proclamation given by the Lord: "Thus shall my church be called in the last days, even The Church of Jesus Christ of Latter-day Saints" (D&C 115:4). He did *not* say, "Thus shall my church be *named.*" He said, "Thus shall my church be *called.*" Members have been cautioned by the Brethren, who wrote: "We feel that some may be misled by the too frequent use of the term

'Mormon Church'" (*Member-Missionary Class, Instructor's Guide* [Salt Lake City: The Church of Jesus Christ of Latter-day Saints, 1982], 2).

38. 2 Nephi 26:33. Additional scripture declares that God "made the world and all things therein, . . . [and] hath made of one blood all nations of men for to dwell on all the face of the earth" (Acts 17:24, 26).

The commandment to love our neighbors without discrimination is certain. But it must not be misunderstood. It applies generally. Selection of a *marriage partner,* on the other hand, involves *specific* and not *general* criteria. After all, one person can be married only to *one* individual.

The probabilities of a successful marriage are known to be much greater if both the husband and wife are united in their religion, language, culture, and ethnic background. Thus, in choosing an eternal companion, wisdom is needed. It's better not to fly in the face of constant head winds. Occasional squalls provide challenge enough. Once marriage vows are taken, absolute fidelity is essential—to the Lord and to one's companion.

39. Acts 3:21.

40. D&C 101:4.

41. D&C 86:9–11.

# THANKS FOR THE COVENANT

I would like to give you a new perspective of gratitude. Against a historical backdrop I should like to paint a mental picture that would allow you more fully to comprehend who you really are. The panorama of history will extend far back. But if you should view your own identity without this broader understanding, such limitation would constitute an unfortunate injustice.

## GOING BACK IN TIME

Everyone no doubt has had at one time or another some sort of identity crisis. On those occasions one has wondered with true introspection, "Who am I really? Why am I here? What am I to do?" To find identity, direction, and purpose, it helps to be reminded of the past.

To get started, answer the following questions:

Who are your parents?

Where is your home?

Are you of Israel?

Are you Hebrew?

Are you related to Abraham? If so, how?

Are you Jewish?

To what countries do you trace your ancestry?

Do you trace any of your ancestry to Egypt?

To find answers, let's go back in a mental time tunnel. Before the world was made, "Jesus Christ, the Great I AM, . . . looked upon the wide expanse of eternity, and all the seraphic hosts of heaven."[1] The Lord had shown Abraham "the intelligences that were organized before the world was; and among all these there were many of the noble and great ones."[2] We are no doubt among those he envisioned.

"And God saw these souls . . . and he said: These I will make my rulers; . . . Abraham, thou art one of them; thou wast chosen before thou wast born."[3] Contemplating the plan to create an earth on which those spirits could dwell, our Heavenly Father said to those about him, "We will prove them herewith, to see if they will do all things whatsoever the Lord their God shall command them."[4]

The Creation was accomplished. The fall of Adam took place that man might be. Dispensations of the gospel were entrusted to Adam, Enoch, Noah, Abraham, and others.[5] Then the Savior of the world was born. Prior to His planned atonement, He ministered among men.

You may recall the conversation the Master had with Jews who questioned His knowledge about Abraham: "Then said the Jews unto [Jesus], Thou art not yet fifty years old, and hast thou seen Abraham?

"Jesus said unto them, Verily, verily I say unto you, Before Abraham was, I am."[6]

"I am" was the name the Lord applied to himself.

## ABRAHAM'S COVENANT

After Abraham withstood the severe trial commanded of God in which Abraham was willing to offer his special son, Isaac, the Lord personally appeared and made a covenant with Abraham. Included were the following assurances:

1. Christ would come through the lineage of Abraham.

2. Abraham's posterity would receive certain lands as an inheritance.[7]

3. All the nations of the earth would be blessed through his seed.[8]

These divine declarations are known as the Abrahamic covenant.

So important were these promises that the Lord personally appeared to Isaac and renewed that covenant.[9] So important were these promises that the Lord personally appeared again to Jacob and reconfirmed that same covenant a third time to a third generation.[10] Jacob's name was changed to Israel,[11] so we may use the terms Jacob and Israel interchangeably.

Well, happily, as men are wont to do, Jacob fell in love. Jacob worked for years for the hand of his intended bride, Rachel. He asked Rachel's father for permission to marry her. But after agreeing, the father veiled faces, switched daughters, and gave his oldest girl, Leah. Her father cited the tradition of giving the hand of his first daughter before allowing the younger daughter to be married.[12]

Later, Rachel and Jacob were permitted to marry. He worked another seven years for her. (That's even longer than waiting for a missionary today!) So great was his affection for Rachel that he described the period as "but a few days, for the love he had [for] her."[13]

Leah bore sons Reuben, Simeon, Levi, and Judah. Meanwhile, Rachel was barren. So desirous was she of having children that she gave to Jacob her handmaiden, Bilhah, as another wife, with the expectation that children born to Bilhah would become Rachel's own, because Rachel owned Bilhah. Bilhah had been given to Rachel as a wedding gift by her father. Bilhah did conceive and gave birth to a son upon Rachel's knees.[14] It was customary for names of babies to be selected by their mothers. "Rachel said, God hath judged me, and hath also heard my voice, and hath given me a son: therefore called she his name Dan."[15] Dan in the Hebrew language means "judge." Rachel wanted Dan judged as though he were her own offspring. Bilhah later bore a second son named Naphtali.[16]

When Leah saw that pattern of surrogate motherhood successfully practiced by her sister, Leah decided to do the same. Her maid, Zilpah, was given to Jacob as a fourth wife, and she bore sons named Gad and Asher.[17] Leah subsequently had two more sons named Issachar and Zebulun.[18]

So Israel had ten sons before Rachel finally conceived and bore a son of her very own. She called his name Joseph.[19] This name had a very special meaning. The word Joseph relates to the Hebrew word *yasaph,* meaning "to add." Rachel wanted all to know that this son was added to sons that she already had through her maid Bilhah. Joseph also relates to the Hebrew word *asaph,* which means "to gather."[20] The name and lineage of Joseph were destined to play an important later role in the gathering of Israel.

In time, Rachel conceived again. As they were traveling from Beth-el in the north to Bethlehem in the south, Rachel went into labor and experienced a fatal complication. Scriptures indicate that it was a particularly hard labor. She endured severe pain. The midwife announced that the baby was a boy and asked for a name. As Rachel was dying, she gave the baby the name Ben-oni,[21] which means "son of my sorrow." Rachel then died and was buried just north of Bethlehem. Her husband was grief-stricken. I suppose he could not bear the thought of being reminded of the death of his beloved Rachel every time the name of the child was mentioned. So Jacob changed the name to Benjamin, which means "son of my right hand."[22] To me, this is one of the most tender love stories in all of holy writ.

## THE BIRTHRIGHT

This history takes on an additional dimension of importance when one considers the Hebrew law of primogeniture, or the birthright. Under this law, for example, if a man had three sons, his estate would be divided not three ways, but four, with a quarter going to each of the three sons and the fourth quarter going to the birthright son. To have the birthright meant power, property, and a measure of wealth to help defray the cost of managing the estate, to take care of any daughters and, who knows, maybe there would be a little left over for an executor's fee.

Being the first son, Reuben held the birthright. But he lost it because he defiled his father's bed. The question is, who was to get the birthright now? Was it to go to the second son, Simeon, or to any of the older boys? No! The Hebrew law of primogeniture required that the birthright go to the first son of the second wife. So the birthright went to Joseph.[23] That's why he was given the coat of many colors. It wasn't because he was a favorite son, necessarily. It was because he was the birthright son. The coat carried that special designation. Of course, this infuriated his ten older brothers. You remember that they angrily sold Joseph into Egypt.

Joseph then married Asenath, and she gave birth to two sons, Manasseh and Ephraim.[24]

Patriarchal blessings were as important then as they are now. When the father of these two sons felt that the time was appropriate for his boys to receive patriarchal blessings, he took them to patriarch Israel, who by that time was elderly. His eyes were described as "dim for age."[25] (I presume he had cataracts.) You

203

remember the story. Israel crossed his hands, put his right hand on the head of the younger Ephraim and his left hand on the head of Manasseh. Joseph tried to correct his father, but Israel persisted in his plan to give the patriarchal blessings in that order. He bestowed upon them blessings of greatness and conferred the birthright upon Ephraim.[26]

## PROMISES FROM THE PAST

What does this ancient history have to do with you and your identity? It has everything to do with your identity. It also relates to the direction your lives may take, your choices, and your challenges. It should even influence your selection of your partner in marriage.

This connection became clear when in our latter day, God the Father and His Son Jesus Christ came to earth. In addition to other actions of eternal consequence, they established once again the Abrahamic covenant, this time through the Prophet Joseph Smith. These are the words of the Lord:

"And as I said unto Abraham concerning the kindreds of the earth, even so I say unto my servant Joseph [Smith]: In thee and in thy seed shall the kindred of the earth be blessed."[27]

The Master conferred upon Joseph Smith priesthood authority and the right to convey blessings of the Abrahamic covenant to others.

Joseph Smith, whose father's name was Joseph, had the same name as Joseph who was sold into Egypt, who millennia before had prophesied of Joseph Smith. This fact is documented in the Book of Mormon.[28] The name *Joseph* carried the connotation both that he was "added" to, and that his mission related to the "gathering" of Israel.

Have the promises of the Abrahamic covenant been fulfilled? Partially. Christ indeed came from the seed of Abraham through the lineage of Judah. That line was entrusted with responsibility for preparing the world for the first coming of the Lord. On the other hand, responsibility for preparation of leadership of the world for the Second Coming of the Lord was assigned to the lineage of Joseph, through Ephraim and Manasseh.

This remarkable fact was foreknown centuries before the birth of the Lord. In the earliest pages of the Book of Mormon, this revelation is recorded:

"Wherefore, our father hath not spoken of our seed alone, but also of all the house of Israel, pointing to the covenant which should be fulfilled in the latter days; which covenant the Lord made to our father Abraham, saying: In thy seed shall all the kindreds of the earth be blessed."[29]

Now, what of the promise of possession of certain lands? Territorial inheritance destined for the sons of Israel provided property in the Holy Land for Reuben, Simeon, Judah, Issachar, Zebulun, Gad, Asher, Dan, Naphtali, and Benjamin.

But where was the inheritance for Joseph? From the Book of Mormon we learn that his inheritance was this land in the American hemisphere[30]—identified as being choice above all other lands.[31] It was choice, but not necessarily from the standpoint of scenery or wealth. It was choice because it was chosen. America was to serve as the repository of sacred records written on metallic plates. It one day was to become the location for the restoration of the gospel. It was to host headquarters of the Lord's restored Church.

Now do you see the importance of your patriarchal blessing? I hope each one of you has obtained one. It is precious. It is personal scripture to you. It declares your special lineage. It reminds you of your linkage with the past. And it will help you realize your future potential. Literally, you can lay claim upon the Lord for fulfillment of those blessings through your faithfulness.

Many of you have already qualified for endowment in the temple, and others will have that great privilege yet in the future. In the temple, with the authority of the sealing power, blessings of the Abrahamic covenant will be conferred. There, we may truly become heirs to all the blessings of Abraham, Isaac, and Jacob.

Each of them had severe trials in life. So will each of us, without exception. Speaking to the Saints of our day, the Lord said:

"They must needs be chastened and tried, even as Abraham, who was commanded to offer up his only son.

"For all those who will not endure chastening . . . cannot be sanctified."[32]

Submissive suffering is just as essential to our sanctification now as it was to patriarchs and prophets before. Knowing who we are helps us to endure our own Abrahamic tests.

## HEIRS TO THE PROMISE

Every man who has received the Melchizedek Priesthood has been foreordained from the foundations of the world for that privilege.[33] Every Latter-day Saint woman has been foredetermined to come at this time to participate in partnership in building up the Church and kingdom of God upon the earth as part of the preparation for the second coming of the Lord.

Now, let's review those questions I asked earlier. Are you of Israel? Absolutely. You are the "Hope of Israel, Zion's army, Children of the promised day."[34] Once you were spirit children in premortal realms with Elohim, Jehovah, Abraham, and other elect rulers-to-be. There you were held in reserve to come forth in this latter day when this great and marvelous work of restoration was to come forth.

Are you Hebrew? Yes, as scriptures define the term. You are

related to Abraham, who was a descendant of the great "Eber" from which the term *Hebrew* was derived.[35]

Are you Jewish? That precious lineage may be claimed if your ancestors are from the loins of Judah. But most of us are of the lineage of Joseph through Ephraim or Manasseh. Joseph's was the lineage selected to pioneer the gathering of Israel, the seed to lead throughout the world in blessing all the nations of the earth.

Missionary work is only the beginning of that blessing. The fulfillment, the consummation, of those blessings comes as those who have entered the waters of baptism perfect their lives to the point that they may enter the holy temple. Receiving an endowment there seals members of the Church to the Abrahamic covenant.

Can you trace your lineage to Egypt? If your patriarchal blessing indicates that you are of the lineage of Joseph, Ephraim, Manasseh, or other descendants of Israel—yes, you may claim Egyptian ancestry.

And, of course, each of you is a child of God, created in His image. And you are disciples of His Beloved Son. If you really comprehend the power of that identity, other elements of your background matter less. Paul described this well. He said:

"For as many of you as have been baptized into Christ have put on Christ.

"There is neither Jew nor Greek, there is neither bond nor free, there is neither male nor female: for ye are all one in Christ Jesus.

"And if ye be Christ's, then are ye Abraham's seed, and heirs according to the promise."[36]

That promise is the promise of the Abrahamic covenant.

The angel Moroni so taught the Prophet Joseph Smith. On 21 September 1823, Moroni appeared to the Prophet, quoting scripture from the fourth chapter of Malachi, "though with a little variation from the way it reads in our Bibles."[37] The difference in text from the Bible is highly significant. You recall it refers to the heart of the fathers being turned to the children, and the heart of the children being turned to the fathers.[38] Joseph Smith tells us that Moroni "quoted the fifth verse thus: Behold, I will reveal unto you the Priesthood, by the hand of Elijah the prophet, before the coming of the great and dreadful day of the Lord.

"He also quoted the next verse differently: And he shall plant in the hearts of the children the promises made to the fathers, and the hearts of the children shall turn to their fathers."[39]

The concept the Prophet was taught emphasized that the hearts of the children will become aware of the promises made to their fathers. Then, with that comprehension, the hearts of the children shall turn to their parents. That includes parents, grandparents, great-great-great-grandparents—including Abraham, Isaac, and Jacob. Once we know who we are and the royal lineage of which we are a part, our actions and our direction in life will be more appropriate to our inheritance.

Now you can better understand this revelation given through the Prophet Joseph Smith. It applies to each one of us. He said:

"Thus saith the Lord unto you, with whom the priesthood hath continued through the lineage of your fathers—

"For ye are lawful heirs, according to the flesh, and have been hid from the world with Christ in God—

"Therefore your life and the priesthood have remained, and must needs remain through you and your lineage until the restoration of all things spoken by the mouths of all the holy prophets since the world began.

"Therefore, blessed are ye if ye continue in my goodness, a

208

light unto the Gentiles, and through this priesthood, a savior unto my people Israel."[40]

The Lord has called you. He has chosen you. You have inherited greatness of transcendent worth.

## "CHILDREN OF THE PROPHETS"

Why are you seeking a higher education? At least two great reasons emerge. One: You are to learn in your youth to keep the commandments of God.[41] There is no other way you can achieve your divine destiny. A prophet said:

"As you have commenced in your youth to look to the Lord your God, even so I hope that you will continue in keeping his commandments; for blessed is he that endureth to the end."[42]

Reason number two: Learn wisdom so that you can render significant service of worth to your fellowmen. How frustrating it would be to have desire only and little or no ability to help people. Prepare your minds and your hands so that you can qualify to serve people and bless their lives. Gain competence that others do not have. That takes work—it takes effort—but it is worth the price.

And for some, a third reason emerges. Here you may fall in love and find your eternal companion. Now with your understanding of the Abrahamic covenant, you may clearly see the importance of marrying within the covenant to obtain all the blessings of the covenant.

Long ago, when Jacob's parents pondered the risk of his dating certain ladies not of covenant Israel, their concern was evident. His mother, Rebekah, said to Isaac:

"If Jacob take a wife . . . such as these which are of the daughters of the land [and not of Israel], what good shall my life do me?"[43] So today your parents and predecessors are pulling and praying for you. Be wise in selecting your companion. Keep courage to be morally clean. Let fidelity and trust distinguish all you do. Don't ever defile your chosen lineage or demean your boundless potential for greatness.

The resurrected Lord told the Nephites: "And behold, ye are the children of the prophets; and ye are of the house of Israel; and ye are of the covenant which the Father made with your fathers, saying unto Abraham: And in thy seed shall all the kindreds of the earth be blessed."[44]

Express gratitude to your Heavenly Father for blessings uniquely yours. Echo in your heart this prayerful plea recorded in the Book of Mormon:

"Take upon you the name of Christ; . . . humble yourselves . . . and worship God, in whatsoever place ye may be in, . . . live in thanksgiving daily, for the many mercies and blessings which he doth bestow upon you."[45]

Gratefully add to your list of blessings thanks for the covenant—the Abrahamic covenant—by which you will be vital and precious participants in God's promise to bless all the nations of the earth through that choice seed.

NOTES

1. D&C 38:1.

2. Abraham 3:22.

3. Abraham 3:23.

4. Abraham 3:25.

5. See Joseph Fielding Smith, *Doctrines of Salvation,* 1:161.

6. John 8:57–58.

7. See Genesis 17; Galatians 3; Abraham 2.

8. See Genesis 17:7; Acts 3:25; 1 Nephi 15:18, 22:9; 3 Nephi 20:25, 27.

9. See Genesis 26:1–4, 24.

10. See Genesis 28, 35:9–13, 48:3–4.

11. See Genesis 35:9–10.

12. See Genesis 29:26.

13. Genesis 29:20.

14. See Genesis 30:3.

15. Genesis 30:6.

16. See Genesis 30:8.

17. See Genesis 30:9–13.

18. See Genesis 35:23.

19. See Genesis 30:24.

20. See Genesis 30:24, footnote 24a in the LDS edition of the King James Version.

21. See Genesis 35:18.

22. See Genesis 35:18.

23. See 1 Chronicles 5:1–2.

24. See Genesis 41:45, 50–52.

25. Genesis 48:10.

26. See Genesis 48:20; see also D&C 133:34.

27. D&C 124:58; see also D&C 110:12.

28. See 2 Nephi 3:6–21.

29. 1 Nephi 15:18.

30. See Ether 13:8.

31. See Ether 1:42; 10:28; 13:2; D&C 38:20.

32. D&C 101:4–5; see also D&C 136:31.

33. See Alma 13:2–3.

34. *Hymns,* no. 259.

35. See Genesis 10:21, 14:13; see also 2 Corinthians 11:22.

36. Galatians 3:27–29.

37. Joseph Smith—History 1:36.

38. See Malachi 4:6.

39. Joseph Smith—History 1:38–39.

40. D&C 86:8–11.

41. See Alma 37:35.

42. Alma 38:2.

43. Genesis 27:46.
44. 3 Nephi 20:25.
45. Alma 34:38.

# SHEPHERDS, LAMBS, AND HOME TEACHERS

S omeone once offered this sage advice: "Survey large fields; cultivate small ones." That seems quite appropriate for home teachers. I, at least, became a better home teacher when my perspective became more global than local. I realized that this would be a better world if everyone had good home teachers. And if such a global outlook is helpful, how much more valuable is an eternal viewpoint, compared with one that is merely mundane.

Faith would increase in the earth and God's everlasting covenant would be established if the Master's desire could be fulfilled. For He expressed the hope "that every man might speak in the name of God the Lord, even the Savior of the world."[1] Every priesthood holder could do this while serving as a home teacher.

As I have surveyed large fields of this planet, my sense of appreciation for home and neighbors nearby has become even more dear. Those feelings of fondness have found meaningful expression in home teaching. Sister Nelson and I are so grateful to have been blessed with home teachers who have given much-needed encouragement to us and our family. Wherever we have lived through the years, we have appreciated home teachers who have observed four hallmarks of effective home teaching. Our home teachers have

• Faithfully kept appointments scheduled in advance;

• Come prepared with brief messages relevant to contemporary need, determined previously in counsel with us as parents;

• Honored our time constraints with visits that were appropriately concise;

• Invoked the Spirit of the Lord upon our family with prayer.

Returning to the broader perspective, in the world today many religious denominations and other well-meaning groups focus attention on concepts such as "wholeness of self," "self-realization," "self-fulfillment," or "self-awareness." But such slogans cause me to wonder if the two great commandments are ignored or forgotten.

Jesus said: "Thou shalt love the Lord thy God with all thy heart, and with all thy soul, and with all thy mind.

"This is the first and great commandment.

"And the second is like unto it, Thou shalt love thy neighbour as thyself."[2]

The two great commandments work in perfect harmony because obedience to the first is manifest by obedience to the second: "When ye are in the service of your fellow beings ye are only in the service of your God."[3]

Rewards for selfless service were revealed by the Lord, who said, "Whosoever will save his life shall lose it: and whosoever will lose his life for my sake shall find it."[4]

Long ago, an enduring standard of interpersonal conduct was set. We know it as the Golden Rule: "All things whatsoever ye would that men should do to you, do ye even so to them."[5]

That principle was established by Jesus, who called Himself the "good shepherd." Appropriately, shepherds were among the first to receive the announcement of His birth.[6] He is our Shepherd and we are the sheep of His fold.[7] Often He used that metaphor in His teachings:

"I am the good shepherd, and know my sheep, and am known of mine.

"As the Father knoweth me, even so know I the Father: and I lay down my life for the sheep."[8]

When the Good Shepherd bade farewell to His disciples, important instructions were given: "Jesus saith to Simon Peter, Simon, son of Jonas, lovest thou me more than these? He saith unto him, Yea, Lord; thou knowest that I love thee. He saith unto him, *Feed* my *lambs.*"[9]

Because the available manuscripts of the New Testament are in Greek, additional insight is gained when the meanings of the words italicized above are studied in the Greek language. The word *feed* comes from the Greek term *bosko,* which means "to nourish or to pasture." The word *lamb* comes from the diminutive term *arnion,* meaning "little lamb."

"[Jesus] saith to him again the second time, Simon, son of Jonas, lovest thou me? He saith unto him, Yea, Lord; thou knowest that I love thee. He saith unto him, *Feed* my *sheep.*"[10]

In this verse, the word *feed* comes from a different term, *poimaino,* which means "to shepherd, to tend, or to care." The word *sheep* comes from the term *probaton,* meaning "mature sheep."

"[Jesus] saith unto him the third time, Simon, son of Jonas, lovest thou me? Peter was grieved because he said unto him the third time, Lovest thou me? And he said unto him, Lord, thou knowest all things; thou knowest that I love thee. Jesus saith unto him, *Feed* my *sheep.*"[11]

In this verse, the word *feed* again comes from the Greek *bosko,* referring to nourishment. The word *sheep* was again translated from the Greek term *probaton,* referring to adult sheep.

215

These three verses, which seem so similar in the English language, really contain three distinct messages in Greek:
- Little lambs need to be nourished in order to grow;
- Sheep need to be tended;
- Sheep also need to be nourished.

Therefore, one of the tangible signs of the restored Church of Jesus Christ would have to be the establishment of an orderly system by which each precious member—young or mature, male or female—might be given the continuing care and nourishment that the Lord decreed for every one of His flock.

That system includes priesthood home teaching. To describe those called to render such service, I like the term, "true undershepherds," as written by Mary B. Wingate in a hymn we love to sing. Her entire text carries a meaningful message:

> Dear to the heart of the Shepherd,
> Dear are the sheep of his fold;
> Dear is the love that he gives them,
> Dearer than silver or gold.
> Dear to the heart of the Shepherd,
> Dear are his "other" lost sheep;
> Over the mountains he follows,
> Over the waters so deep. . . .
>
> Dear to the heart of the Shepherd,
> Dear are the lambs of his fold;
> Some from the pastures are straying,
> Hungry and helpless and cold.
> See, the Good Shepherd is seeking,
> Seeking the lambs that are lost,
> Bringing them in with rejoicing,
> Saved at such infinite cost. . . .

Dear to the heart of the Shepherd,
Dear are the "ninety and nine";
Dear are the sheep that have wandered
Out in the desert to pine.
Hark! he is earnestly calling,
Tenderly pleading today:
"Will you not seek for my lost ones,
Off from my shelter astray?" . . .

Green are the pastures inviting;
Sweet are the waters and still.
Lord, we will answer thee gladly,
"Yes, blessed Master, we will!
Make us thy true undershepherds;
Give us a love that is deep.
Send us out into the desert,
Seeking thy wandering sheep."

Out in the desert they wander,
Hungry and helpless and cold;
Off to the rescue we'll hasten,
Bringing them back to the fold.[12]

No doubt Mary B. Wingate's text was inspired by the Savior's parable of the lost sheep, recorded in the New Testament: "What man of you, having an hundred sheep, if he lose one of them, doth not leave the ninety and nine in the wilderness, and go after that which is lost, until he find it?"[13]

When the Prophet Joseph Smith rendered his inspired translation of that verse, he wrote, "What man of you having a hundred sheep, if he lose one of them, doth not leave the ninety and nine, and go into the wilderness after that which is lost, until he find it?"[14]

The concept that the man would leave his normal surroundings and "go into the wilderness" in order to rescue is very compelling to me. What an example for home teachers!

Recently I spoke with a heartbroken stake president who tearfully told me that one of his own adult children had lost faith in the Lord and had strayed from the Church. He said, "I extend a helping hand to less-active members in my stake more searchingly now, hoping that somewhere someone might do the same and find and feed my lost one."

One who rescues a lamb of the Lord brings joy to many: "And when he hath found [the lost sheep], he layeth it on his shoulders, rejoicing.

"And when he cometh home, he calleth together his friends and neighbours, saying unto them, Rejoice with me; for I have found my sheep which was lost."[15]

### DOCTRINAL FOUNDATION FOR HOME TEACHING

The doctrinal foundation for home teaching has been instituted by the Lord. In the revelation on Church organization and government in Doctrine and Covenants section 20, these directions are recorded:

*"The duty of the elders, priests, teachers, deacons, and members of the church of Christ . . .*

"[Is] to teach, expound, exhort, baptize, and watch over the church."[16]

"The priest's duty is to preach, teach, . . .

"And visit the house of each member, and exhort them to pray vocally and in secret and attend to all family duties."[17]

"[An elder is to] visit the house of each member, exhorting them to pray vocally and in secret and attend to all family duties.

"In all these duties the priest is to assist the elder if occasion requires."[18]

"The teacher's duty is to watch over the church always, and be with and strengthen them;

"And see that there is no iniquity in the church, neither hardness with each other, neither lying, backbiting, nor evil speaking;

"And see that the church meet together often, and also see that all the members do their duty."[19]

Additional instructions were given regarding the pairing of companions in the work of the Lord:

"If any man among you be strong in the Spirit, let him take with him him that is weak, that he may be edified in all meekness, that he may become strong also.

"Therefore, take with you those who are ordained unto the lesser priesthood, and send them before you to make appointments, and to prepare the way."[20]

As I reflect upon my own opportunities for Church service in the several cities where Sister Nelson and I have lived, few experiences have been more gratifying than those as a home teacher. Some of the brothers and sisters we first met through those contacts, who at one time may not have been very active in the Church, have since been called to serve as stake presidents, mission presidents, auxiliary presidents, and temple presidents and matrons. They and members of their families have become some of our dearest friends.

But home teaching requires energy. I remember times when I was so exhausted from the demands of difficult days in the surgical operating room (in addition to duties relating to family needs and other Church responsibilities) that the prospects of spending evening hours in home teaching were not always anticipated eagerly. Almost without exception, however, I can say that I returned home more invigorated and happy than when I left. I often told Sister Nelson that rewards for a home teacher were not remote; they were immediate, at least for me.

Besides, in this world of gluttony and greed, there is a certain satisfaction that comes from rendering service to others purely because of love and not for pay. I think the Apostle Peter felt that same exhilaration when he wrote:

"Feed the flock of God which is among you, taking the oversight thereof, not by constraint, but willingly; not for filthy lucre, but of a ready mind;

"Neither as being lords over God's heritage, but being ensamples to the flock.

"And when the chief Shepherd shall appear, ye shall receive a crown of glory that fadeth not away."[21]

I recognize that it takes time to develop the discipline and desire to prioritize concern for others ahead of one's personal interests. That ennobling transition begins when one makes the baptismal covenant:

"Now, as ye are desirous to come into the fold of God, and to be called his people, and are willing to bear one another's burdens, that they may be light;

"Yea, and are willing to mourn with those that mourn; yea, and comfort those that stand in need of comfort, and to stand as witnesses of God at all times and in all things, . . .

"Now I say unto you, if this be the desire of your hearts, what have you against being baptized in the name of the Lord, as a witness before him that ye have entered into a covenant with him, that ye will serve him and keep his commandments, that he may pour out his Spirit more abundantly upon you?"[22]

Home teaching opportunities provide a means by which an important aspect of character may be developed: love of service above self. We become more like the Savior, who has challenged us to emulate His example: "What manner of men ought ye to be? Verily I say unto you, even as I am."[23]

Each individual who sincerely strives to become more like

the Good Shepherd will be blessed. His promise and challenge are real: "Thou art my servant; and I covenant with thee that thou shalt have eternal life; and thou shalt serve me and go forth in my name, and shalt gather together my sheep."[24]

Remembering that the Savior is our exemplar, picture in your mind a little lamb being carried across His shoulders, as you read His divine directive:

"Ye know the things that ye must do in my church; for the works which ye have seen me do that shall ye also do; for that which ye have seen me do even that shall ye do;

"Therefore, if ye do these things blessed are ye, for ye shall be lifted up at the last day."[25]

The following admonition was given by President Ezra Taft Benson:

"The Good Shepherd gave His life for the sheep—for you and me—for us all (see John 10:17–18). The symbolism of the Good Shepherd is not without parallel in the Church today. The sheep need to be led by watchful shepherds. Too many are wandering. Some are being enticed away by momentary distractions. Others have become completely lost. . . .

"With a shepherd's care, our new members, those newly born into the gospel, must be nurtured by attentive fellowshipping as they increase in gospel knowledge and begin living new standards. Such attention will help to ensure that they will not return to old habits. With a shepherd's loving care, our young people, our young lambs, will not be as inclined to wander. And if they do, the crook of a shepherd's staff, a loving arm and an understanding heart, will help to retrieve them. With a shepherd's care, many of those who are now independent of the flock can still be reclaimed. Many who have married outside the Church and have assumed the life-styles of the world may respond to an invitation to return to the fold."[26]

As I foresee the troublesome times that lie ahead—when deepening trials and testing shall be thrust upon members of the Church[27]—the gentle caring of compassionate home teachers may literally save spiritual lives.

"For what shepherd is there among you having many sheep doth not watch over them, that the wolves enter not and devour his flock? . . .

"And now I say unto you that the good shepherd doth call after you; and if you will hearken unto his voice he will bring you into his fold, and ye are his sheep; and he commandeth you that ye suffer no ravenous wolf to enter among you, that ye may not be destroyed."[28]

Personal security through the travails of life cannot be guaranteed by wealth, fame, or governmental programs. But it can come from doing the will of the Lord, whose instructions are given to bring spiritual protection to His Saints. His merciful commandments, with undergirding and overarching power to sustain all natural law, tenderly allow gentle hands to guard His children well.

The Good Shepherd lovingly cares for all sheep of His fold, and we are His true undershepherds. Our privilege is to bear His love and to add our own love to friends and neighbors—feeding, tending, and nurturing them—as the Savior would have us do. By so doing, we evidence one of the godly characteristics of His restored Church upon the earth.

NOTES

1. D&C 1:20.

2. Matthew 22:37–39; see also D&C 59:6.

3. Mosiah 2:17.

4. Matthew 16:25; see also 10:39.

5. Matthew 7:12.

6. See Luke 2:8–18.

7. See Psalm 23:1.

8. John 10:14–15; see also verses 11, 27; D&C 50:44.

9. John 21:15; emphasis added.

10. John 21:16; emphasis added.

11. John 21:17; emphasis added.

12. *Hymns,* no. 221; emphasis added.

13. Luke 15:4.

14. JST, Luke 15:4.

15. Luke 15:5–6.

16. D&C 20:38, 42.

17. D&C 20:46–47.

18. D&C 20:51–52.

19. D&C 20:53–55.

20. D&C 84:106–7.

21. 1 Peter 5:2–4.

22. Mosiah 18:8–10; see also D&C 20:37.

23. 3 Nephi 27:27; see also John 13:15; 1 Peter 2:21; 3 Nephi 18:6, 16.

24. Mosiah 26:20.

25. 3 Nephi 27:21–22.

26. *The Teachings of Ezra Taft Benson* (Salt Lake City: Bookcraft, 1988), 231–32.

27. See D&C 1:12–23; 101:4–5.

28. Alma 5:59–60.

# CONSTANCY AMID CHANGE

O ur youth are wonderful and especially able to ask thoughtful questions. A few years ago, I had a conversation with
"Ruth" and "John." Ruth opened the discussion. With a sigh, she
lamented, "Our world is constantly changing, isn't it?"

"Yes," I replied, "ever since its creation—geologically and
geographically. And its populations are changing—politically and
spiritually. You might ask your grandparents about life when they
were your age and discover their thoughts."

"Oh, I already have," Ruth continued. "My grandpa summa-
rized his opinion with a clever quip: 'Give me the good old
days—plus penicillin.'"

Then John expressed deep concern. "Continually changing
conditions make the future shaky for us," he said. "It's kind of
scary. We seem to be standing on shifting sand."

Together they asked, "What can we trust? Is anything constant that will *not* change as we grow older?"

To that question I responded with an emphatic, "Yes! Many
things!" Ruth and John are typical of many today who seek for
unchanging constants in a changing world. Through the years,
prophets and Apostles have spoken of many unchanging con-

stants.[1] I will group some of these constants into three categories: heavenly personages, plans, and principles.

## PERSONAGES

Our Heavenly Father has a glorified body of flesh and bone, inseparably connected with His spirit.[2] Scriptures state that He is "infinite and eternal, from everlasting to everlasting the same unchangeable God."[3]

His Beloved Son, Jesus Christ, is our Savior and the chief cornerstone of our religion.[4] "He is the life and the light of the world."[5] "There shall be no other name . . . nor any other way . . . whereby salvation can come unto the children of men, only in and through the name of Christ, the Lord Omnipotent."[6]

Another personage is the Holy Ghost, whose enduring influence transcends time. Scripture assures that "the Holy Ghost shall be thy *constant* companion, and thy scepter an *unchanging* scepter of righteousness and truth; and thy dominion shall be an *everlasting* dominion, and without compulsory means it shall flow unto thee *forever* and ever."[7]

Brothers and sisters, these Heavenly Beings love you. Their love is as constant as is the greatest love of earthly parents.

But there is another personage about whom you should be reminded. Satan also exists and seeks "that all men might be miserable like unto himself."[8]

## PLANS

A great council in heaven was once convened, in which it seems that all of us participated.[9] There our Heavenly Father announced His plan. Scriptures refer to this plan of God[10] by many names. Perhaps out of deference to the sacred name of Deity, or to depict its broad scope, it is also called the plan of happiness,[11] the plan of salvation,[12] the plan of redemption,[13] the plan of restoration,[14] the plan of mercy,[15] the plan of deliverance,[16] and the everlasting gospel.[17] Prophets have used these terms interchangeably. Regardless of designation, the enabling essence of the plan is the atonement of Jesus Christ. As it is central to the plan,[18] we should try to comprehend the meaning of the Atonement. Before we can comprehend it, though, we must understand the fall of Adam. And before we can fully appreciate the Fall, we must first comprehend the Creation. These three events—the Creation, the Fall, and the Atonement—are three preeminent pillars of God's plan, and they are doctrinally interrelated.

**The Creation.** The creation of the earth was a preparatory part of our Father's plan. Then "the Gods went down to organize man in their own image, . . . male and female to form they them.

"And the Gods said: We will bless them."[19] And bless us they did, with a plan that would give us physical bodies of our very own.

Adam and Eve were the first people to live upon the earth.[20] They were different from the plant and animal life that had been created previously. Adam and Eve were children of God. Their bodies of flesh and bone were made in the express image of God's. In that state of innocence, they were not yet mortal. They could have had no children,[21] were not subject to death, and could have lived in Eden's garden forever.[22] Thus, we might speak of the Creation in terms of a *paradisiacal* creation.

If that state had persisted, you and I would still be stranded among the heavenly host as unborn sons and daughters of God.[23] "The great plan of [happiness] would have been frustrated."[24]

**The Fall.** To bring the plan of happiness to fruition, God issued to Adam and Eve the first commandment ever given to mankind. It was a commandment to beget children.[25] A law was explained to them. Should they eat from "the tree of the knowledge of good and evil,"[26] their bodies would change; mortality and eventual death would come upon them.[27] But partaking of that fruit was prerequisite to their parenthood.[28]

While I do not fully understand all the biochemistry involved, I do know that their physical bodies did change; blood began to circulate in their bodies. Adam and Eve thereby became mortal. Happily for us, they could also beget children and fulfill the purposes for which the world was created. Happily for them, "the Lord said unto Adam [and Eve[29]]: Behold I have forgiven thee thy transgression in the Garden of Eden."[30] We and all mankind are forever blessed because of Eve's great courage and wisdom. By partaking of the fruit first, she did what needed to be done. Adam was wise enough to do likewise. Accordingly, we could speak of the fall of Adam in terms of a *mortal* creation, because "Adam fell that men might be."[31]

Other blessings came to us through the Fall. It activated two closely coupled additional gifts from God, nearly as precious as life itself—agency and accountability. We became "free to choose liberty and eternal life . . . or to choose captivity and death."[32] Freedom of choice cannot be exercised without accountability for choices made.[33]

**The Atonement.** Now we come to the third pillar of God's plan—the Atonement. Just as Adam and Eve were not to live forever in the Garden of Eden, so our final destination was not to be planet earth. We were to return to our heavenly home.

Given that reality, still another change was necessary. An infinite atonement was required to redeem Adam, Eve, and all of their posterity. That atonement must enable our physical bodies to be resurrected and changed[34] to a bloodless form, no longer liable to disease, deterioration, or death.

According to eternal law, that atonement required a personal sacrifice by an immortal being not subject to death. Yet He must die and take up His own body again. The Savior was the only one who could accomplish this. From His mother He inherited power to die. From His Father He obtained power over death. The Redeemer so explained:

"I lay down my life, that I might take it again.

"No man taketh it from me, but I lay it down of myself. I have power to lay it down, and I have power to take it again."[35]

The Lord declared that "this is my work and my glory—to bring to pass the immortality and eternal life of man."[36] He who had created the earth came into mortality to fulfill the will of His Father[37] and all prophecies of His atonement.[38] And His atonement redeems every soul from penalties of personal transgression, on the condition of repentance.[39]

Thus, we might speak of the Atonement in terms of the *immortal* creation. "For as in Adam all die, even so in Christ shall all be made alive."[40]

I have recounted the importance of the Creation, the Fall, and the Atonement, knowing that parents are accountable to teach these precepts of God's plan to their children.[41]

Before leaving our discussion of unchanging plans, however, we need to remember that the adversary sponsors a cunning plan of his own.[42] It invariably attacks God's first commandment for husband and wife to beget children. It tempts with tactics that include infidelity, unchastity, and other abuses of procreative power. Satan's band would trumpet choice, but mute accountability. Nevertheless, his capacity has long been limited, "for he knew not the mind of God."[43]

## PRINCIPLES

Unchanging principles are so because they come from our unchanging Heavenly Father. Try as they might, no parliament or congress could ever repeal the law of earth's gravity or amend the Ten Commandments. Those laws are constant. All laws of nature and of God are part of the everlasting gospel. Thus, there are many unchanging principles. Space will permit consideration of only a few.

**Priesthood.** One of them is that of the priesthood. The Prophet Joseph Smith taught that "the Priesthood is an everlasting principle, and existed with God from eternity, and will to eternity, without beginning of days or end of years."[44]

We know that "the Priesthood was first given to Adam; he obtained the First Presidency, and held the keys of it from generation to generation. He obtained it in the Creation, before the world was formed."[45]

Scriptures certify that the priesthood has continued and will continue "through the lineage of [the] fathers."[46] Ordination to its offices has timeless implication as well. Tenure in priesthood office may extend into postmortal realms. For example, scriptures declare that one ordained as a high priest may be a high priest forever.[47] Promised *blessings* of the priesthood extend to men, women, and children throughout the world and may endure forever.[48]

The use of the priesthood is carefully controlled according to conditions established by the Lord, who said:

"No power or influence can or ought to be maintained by virtue of the priesthood, only by persuasion, by long-suffering, by gentleness and meekness, and by love unfeigned."[49]

"That [the rights of the priesthood] may be conferred upon [men], it is true; but when [they] undertake to cover [their] sins, or to gratify [their] pride, [their] vain ambition, or to exercise control or dominion or compulsion upon the souls of the children of men, in any degree of unrighteousness, . . . the Spirit of

229

the Lord is grieved; and when it is withdrawn, Amen to the priesthood or the authority of that man."[50]

While the priesthood is an everlasting principle, those privileged to exercise its authority must maintain themselves daily as worthy vessels.

**Moral Law.** Another unchanging principle is that of divine or moral law. Transgression of moral law brings retribution; obedience to it brings blessings "immutable and unchangeable."[51] Blessings are always predicated upon obedience to law.[52] So the Church teaches us to embrace the right and to renounce the wrong—that we might have joy.[53]

The Savior and His servants[54] do not speak words of complacency but teach what people need to know. Through the ages, history attests that contemporary critics have pressed Church leaders to modify a decree of the Lord.[55] But such is eternal law, and it cannot be altered. Not even for His Beloved Son could God change the law that required the Atonement. Divine doctrines cannot be squeezed into compact molds to make them fit fashionable patterns of the day. Nor can they be fully expressed on a bumper sticker.

**Judgment.** Another unchanging principle is that of our eventual judgment. Each of us will be judged according to our individual works and the desires of our hearts.[56] We will not be required to pay the debt of any other. Our eventual placement in the celestial, terrestrial, or telestial kingdom will not be determined by chance. The Lord has prescribed unchanging requirements for each. We can know what the scriptures teach and pattern our lives accordingly.[57]

**Divine Commandments.** Other unchanging principles include divine commandments—even those that seem to be temporal. Tithing, for example, is not temporal (or temporary); it is an everlasting principle. The Lord said:

"Those who have thus been tithed shall pay one-tenth of all their interest annually; and this shall be a standing law unto them *forever.*"[58]

We know that tithe payers shall not be burned at the Second Coming.[59]

**Truth.** Another unchanging principle is that of truth. Scripture reminds us that "the truth abideth forever and ever."[60] Even though one's understanding of the truth may be fragmentary, truth itself does not change. Everlasting truth and wisdom come from the Lord. The first truth ever taught to man came directly from Deity. From generation to generation, God has given additional light. Whether truth comes from a laboratory of science or directly by revelation, truth is embraced by the gospel.

**Family.** One more everlasting principle is the family. A family can be together forever. Though each of us will pass through the doors of death, the timing of that departure is less important than is the preparation for eternal life. Part of that preparation includes service in the Church. It is not to be a burden but a blessing to a family. The Lord said, "Thy duty is unto the church forever, and this because of thy family."[61]

Ruth, John, and each of us will more fully understand that concept in light of this scriptural promise:

"If a man marry a wife by my word, which is my law, and by the new and everlasting covenant, and it is sealed unto them . . . [they] shall inherit thrones, kingdoms, principalities, and powers, dominions, . . . exaltation and glory in all things, . . . which glory shall be a fulness and a continuation of the seeds forever and ever."[62]

A promise like that is worth your personal effort and endurance.

Constancy amid change is assured by heavenly personages, plans, and principles. Our trust can be safely anchored to them.

231

They provide peace, eternal progression, hope, freedom, love, and joy to all who will be guided by them. They are true—now and forever.

## NOTES

1. For example, see Albert E. Bowen, *Constancy Amid Change,* (Salt Lake City: Deseret News Press, 1944); N. Eldon Tanner, *Ensign,* November 1979, 80–82.

2. See D&C 93:33; 130:22.

3. D&C 20:17; see also Psalm 100:5; Mormon 9:19; Moroni 8:18; D&C 84:102.

4. See Ephesians 2:20.

5. Alma 38:9; see also Mosiah 16:9; 3 Nephi 9:18; 11:11; Ether 4:12; D&C 10:70; 11:28; 12:9; 34:2; 39:2; 45:7.

6. Mosiah 3:17; see also Acts 4:12; 2 Nephi 25:20; Mosiah 5:8; Alma 38:9; Helaman 5:9; D&C 18:23.

7. D&C 121:46; emphasis added.

8. 2 Nephi 2:27; see also 2 Nephi 2:18; Alma 41:4.

9. See *Teachings of the Prophet Joseph Smith,* 348–49, 365.

10. See 2 Nephi 9:13; Alma 34:9.

11. See Alma 42:8, 16.

12. See Jarom 1:2; Alma 24:14; 42:5; Moses 6:62.

13. See Jacob 6:8; Alma 12:25–33; 17:16; 18:39; 22:13; 29:2; 34:16, 31; 39:18; 42:11–13.

14. See Alma 41:2.

15. See Alma 42:15, 31; 2 Nephi 9:6.

16. See 2 Nephi 11:5.

17. See Revelation 14:6; D&C 27:5; 36:5; 68:1; 77:8, 9, 11; 79:1; 84:103; 88:103; 99:1; 101:22, 39; 106:2; 109:29, 65; 124:88; 128:17; 133:36; 135:3, 7; 138:19, 25; Joseph Smith—History 1:34.

18. See *Teachings of the Prophet Joseph Smith,* 121.

19. Abraham 4:27–28.

20. See Genesis 3:20; 1 Nephi 5:11; Moses 4:26.

21. See 2 Nephi 2:23; Moses 5:11.

22. See 2 Nephi 2:22.

23. See D&C 38:1; Abraham 3:22–23.

24. See Alma 42:5; see also D&C 138:56.

25. See Genesis 1:28; Moses 2:28; Abraham 4:28.

26. Genesis 2:17.

27. See Moses 3:17; Abraham 5:13.

28. See Moses 5:11.

29. The Lord "called *their* name Adam" (Genesis 5:2; Moses 6:9; emphasis added).

30. Moses 6:53.

31. 2 Nephi 2:25; see also Moses 6:48.

32. 2 Nephi 2:27.

33. See D&C 101:78; 134:1.

34. See 1 Corinthians 15:51–53; 3 Nephi 28:8.

35. John 10:17–18.

36. Moses 1:39.

37. See 3 Nephi 27:13.

38. See Romans 5:11; 2 Nephi 25:16; Jacob 4:11, 12; Mosiah 3:5–11, 16, 18–19; 4:2; Alma 21:9; 22:14; 34:8; 36:17; Helaman 5:9; Moroni 7:41; Moses 7:45.

39. See D&C 138:19.

40. 1 Corinthians 15:22.

41. See Moses 6:57–62.

42. See 2 Nephi 9:28.

43. Moses 4:6.

44. *Teachings of the Prophet Joseph Smith,* 157; see also Exodus 40:15; Numbers 25:13; Alma 13:7.

45. *Teachings of the Prophet Joseph Smith,* 157.

46. D&C 86:8; see also D&C 84:6–17; 107:40; Abraham 1:2–4.

47. See Alma 13:9, 14.

48. See Genesis 17:1–7; 22:16–18; 26:3–4; 28:13–14; Isaiah 2:2–3; 1 Nephi 15:18; Alma 29:8; D&C 124:58; 132:47; Abraham 2:11.

49. D&C 121:41.

50. D&C 121:37.

51. D&C 104:2.

52. See D&C 130:20–21.

53. See 2 Nephi 2:25.

54. See D&C 1:38.

55. For examples, see 1 Samuel 8:4–7; Matthew 7:21; Luke 6:46; 3 Nephi 14:21.

56. See D&C 137:9.

57. See John 14:2; 1 Corinthians 15:40–41; D&C 76:50–119; 98:18.

58. D&C 119:4; emphasis added.

59. See D&C 64:23; 85:3.

60. D&C 1:39; see also Psalm 100:5; 117:2.

61. D&C 23:3; see also D&C 126:3.

62. D&C 132:19.

# INDEX

235